THE DEPICTIVE IMAGE

THE

Depictive

IMAGE

Metaphor and Literary Experience

PHILLIP   STAMBOVSKY

The University of Massachusetts Press

Amherst

1988

Copyright © 1988 by The University of Massachusetts Press
All rights reserved
Printed in the United States of America
Set in Linoterm Bodoni
Printed by Thomson-Shore and bound by
John H. Dekker & Sons

Library of Congress Cataloging-in-Publication Data

Stambovsky, Phillip, 1952–
The depictive image : metaphor and literary
experience / Phillip Stambovsky.
        p.   cm.
Bibliography: p.
Includes index.
ISBN 0–87023–614–8 (alk. paper)
1. Metaphor. 2. Literature—Philosophy. 3. Imagination.
I. Title.
PN228.M4S73   1988   808—dc19   87–28802
                                                CIP

British Library Cataloguing in Publication data are available

Acknowledgments for permission to reprint selections from material
under copyright are given on the last printed page.

C O N T E N T S

ACKNOWLEDGMENTS

I owe thanks to Walker Gibson who helped to guide my research at the outset and who critiqued the initial draft of what became parts of the first and third chapters of this book. The series of revisions and expansions that followed resulted in an extended essay, sections of which I read at an annual meeting of the American Society for Aesthetics, Eastern Division, in 1985. Presentation before that forum led to still further development and clarification of my views.

As I began to organize it into book form, the work benefitted greatly from the suggestions and discerning criticism of Arthur Kinney and Gareth Matthews. I am also indebted to Mark Johnson and Marlena C. Corcoran for their valuable analyses of the penultimate version of the manuscript. In addition, I wish to thank Robert Keefe for reading and commenting on the work and Richard Martin of the University of Massachusetts Press for his generous attentiveness and enthusiastic support. Finally, I am grateful to Pam Wilkinson for her expertise in helping to prepare the manuscript for publication.

THE DEPICTIVE IMAGE

INTRODUCTION

Noting that "Literary theory, as traditionally conceived, seems ineluctably antagonistic to literary experience," a recent essay on theory and practice in literary studies calls for the formulation of a conceptual language that would integrate literary theory and critical practice.[1] In the burgeoning scholarship on metaphor, the disparity between theory and literary critical practice is particularly acute. Doubtless part of the reason for the antagonism is that the majority of influential theorists of metaphor are not literary critics but philosophers, linguists, and rhetoricians.[2] Predictably enough, inquiries into the metaphoric process pursued by the latter generally involve frames of analysis that do not account for the distinctively *literary experience* in which literary metaphors occur. Whatever the ultimate source of difficulty, however, theories of metaphor by and large fail to elucidate the *how* of literary metaphor in such a way as to reveal the motive for metaphor—that is, few investigate the aspects of literary experience that attest to the unique communicative power that artists instinctively turn to metaphor to attain.

Endeavoring to contribute to a rapprochement between theory and practical criticism in literature, between interpretation and understanding, the present study outlines an experiential approach to literary metaphor, one that takes into account both prediscursive and analytic experiences as they bear on the apprehension of literary metaphor. The view elaborated here is that literary metaphor depicts the themes that occasion it, conveying meaning imagistically by rendering it presentational.

In literary art the term *theme* commonly refers to an abstract concept that is presented concretely through action and imagery. By stating that

3

themes "occasion" literary metaphor, I emphasize not only that action and imagery are conceptually significant but that they arise in terms of a determinate conceptual context to which their intelligibility is keyed.

I take a functional view of theme, which if it is to be conceived as it operates in literary experience, cannot be abstracted from its imagistic presentation in literature. An idea that is not presented in the action and imagery of a literary work can hardly qualify as a literary theme. In what follows, I assert that in literature themes make ideas significant, that themes are concepts become narrative, and that they communicate thought with sensuous immediacy through their presentational rendering as narrative events. By stressing these points, I aim to focus attention on functions of the presentational aspects of literary themes, that is, their imagistic, actional, and hence dramatic character. On the other hand, when alluding to imagery as a formal constituent of literary themes, to concepts as the *emplotment* of thematic trajectories, or to themes as an organizing principle of the presentational in literary experience, I am concentrating on the purely formal aspects and efficacy of ideas as they inform a literary work.

Theorists whose explanation of metaphor is more explicitly structuralist than one based on the character of presentational experience tend to assume that it involves predication of some sort. Max Black, for instance, conceives the metaphoric process as the formation of a set of implications that are suggested by a "focal" word or phrase and that get predicated of (Black's verb is "fit") the "primary subject," i.e., the setting or "frame" of the metaphor. Eschewing formulaic schemas such as Black's, Paul Ricoeur regards metaphor as "an unexpected or 'impertinent' predication." He postulates that metaphor is a case of "semantic impertinence," a deviation of meaning "on the predicative level" that occurs in the context of discourse as a whole rather than merely in terms of the word or the sentence.[3]

Despite the widely held assumption that it is a key element of the metaphoric—including the literary metaphoric—process, predication is in fact a logical function of deliberative construal and as such is *at a conscious remove* from the experience of literary metaphor, which in the first instance is *intuitive*.[4] Approaches to metaphor that attribute predication to the metaphoric process, and so consider it amenable to "literal" paraphrase, confuse explanations or interpretative inference with the phenomenological data of awareness that explanations are supposed to clarify.[5] In the present work, however, predication is associated strictly with exegesis and is not invoked as an explanation of how literary metaphor operates in the medium of presentational awareness.

In addition to its phenomenological orientation, the view of literary metaphor developed in this inquiry is pragmatic. The way that language is *used* is understood as constitutive of the context in which metaphor is intelligible in the first place, a context that includes "the speaker, his audience, and the non-linguistic setting."[6] When the speaker is not actually present, as is usually the case in literary experience, the reader enacts the speaker's role—something that can be said to take place even in his presence to the degree that the audience "makes out" the speaker and whom he thinks he is addressing, as well as what he is saying.

Defining metaphor in light of its pragmatics is linked to a general development traced by W. V. Quine in the history of empirical thought. Quine notes that "defining a symbol in use . . . [is] an advance over the impossible term-by-term empiricism of Locke and Hume. . . . The statement," Quine goes on to explain, "rather than the term, came with Bentham to be recognized as the unit accountable to an empiricist critique." Advocating a radically more comprehensive frame of meaning as the primary unit of empirical analysis, Quine suggests that "even in taking the statement as unit we have drawn our grid too finely. The unit of empirical significance is the whole of science."[7]

The trend in recent thinking on metaphor is a function of, and thus not surprisingly recapitulates, the development in intellectual history that Quine points to and to which he has significantly contributed. As Mark Johnson states in his introduction to *Philosophical Perspectives on Metaphor* (1981):[8]

> The last few years . . . compelled general acknowledgment that any adequate account of metaphor must explain the complex interaction of both extrasentential and extralinguistic knowledge. (P. 23)

Ricoeur's studies in *The Rule of Metaphor* (1977) develop along a pattern identical to that which Quine finds in the evolution of empiricism and attest to the shift in metaphor theory that Johnson notes. For Ricoeur the "unit of empirical significance" with respect to metaphor is not the word or the sentence but the universe of discourse, the equivalent of Quine's "whole of science."

The depictive theory propounded in what follows is predicated on extralinguistic knowledge, although of a different sort than the compositional logic Ricoeur has in mind. As a datum of literary experience, the depictive image is conceived as a phenomenological presence that acquires its definition through the course of the articulation of the particular themes that give rise to it and which it amplifies. The depictive image is thus understood as a field phenomenon whose form is not definitively delimited by any sort of structure, linguistic or otherwise. The metaphoric process on this view involves the apprehension of depictive imagery that operates as a presentational dynamic in the unfolding of literary themes that occurs in the medium of the reader's consciousness.

Every inquiry into metaphor is concerned with what metaphor is and what it does. Few, however, attempt to ground the presuppositions informing the way that they construe the metaphoric process in the experiential context in which literary metaphor depicts meaning. The chapters that follow aim to do precisely that.

Chapter 1 is largely a critical review of the most influential thinking in the history of the idea of metaphor, and it begins with a consideration of Aristotle's pronouncements on the topic. Although, as we shall see, the views of the originator of metaphor theory have been incisively criticized, they remain the source of underlying assumptions about the metaphoric process that inform most of the current linguistic and semiotic theories. After appraising in section 1 the Aristotelian conceptions of metaphor as comparison, substitution, transfer, and analogy, I turn in the second section to the interaction theories of I. A. Richards and Max Black. The first and one of the few genuine breaks with the Aristotelian tradition in the twentieth century,[9] interactionism is evaluated vis-à-vis the charges of its critics and in the context of a dramatic metaphor in Allen Tate's powerful "Death of Little Boys." The third section of chapter 1 takes up the controversion, verbal-opposition, iconic signification, and supervenience (intuitionist) theories of metaphor. While less seminal than Aristotelian and interaction views, these approaches are among the most influential in the recent scholarship. Section 4 shifts from the theories of particular thinkers to an exploration of the role of context in the metaphoric process. While no theorist of metaphor has worked out a specifically contextual approach, every hypothesis of note on the mechanism of metaphor emphasizes the centrality of contextual factors. Subtitled "Notes Toward a Contextual Theory of Metaphor," this section culls the observations of a number of scholars on the function of context in metaphoric meaning and synthesizes a cogent contextual perspective on metaphor. The pragmatic implications of this approach are then considered in a discussion of the cardinal metaphor whose center is "the flight in me" in George Herbert's "Easter Wings." Chapter 1 concludes with a review of the basic theoretical inadequacies inherent in the predominant accounts of metaphor and stresses the need in any satisfactory view for an explicitly articulated context to afford a determinate sense of the *meaning* of metaphorical meaning.

The phenomenological orientation of the present study, along with its specific concern with literary metaphor, makes literary experience the clear choice as the appropriate context for the analysis of literary metaphoric meaning. Accordingly, chapter 2 develops a phenomenology of literary experience that serves as a frame of reference for the construal of literary metaphor as a depictive image. Opening with a discussion of the phenomenological character of literary experience as it contrasts with analytic thinking, section 1 appeals to the insights of Ernst Cassirer, Jean-Paul Sartre, Rudolph Arnheim, and Northrop Frye, among others, in asserting the primacy of presentational awareness in literary experience. Section 2 introduces the concept of the *presentational immediacy of literary experience*, a notion derived from Alfred North Whitehead's epistemological analysis of symbolism in *Symbolism* and *Process and Reality*. A combination of "pure presentational immediacy" and "causal efficacy," the presentational immediacy of literary experience is what Whitehead would have classified as a "mixed" mode of perception. Phenomenologically speaking, it is nevertheless first-order, *intuitive*, experience, and the perceptions of Benedetto Croce, Edmund Husserl, Maurice Merleau-Ponty, and others are adduced in support of the contention that presentational awareness is intuitive and thereby of epistemological primacy. The presentational immediacy of literary experience is a function of a reader's participation in the creation of textual meaning that is manifest in literary experience, and section 2 concludes by emphasizing this "mimesis of literary experience,"[10] this collaborative—indeed per-formative and dramatic—dimension of the reader's literary involvement with a text. Chapter 2 closes with a summary of the theory of literary experience that I expound in the first two sections of the chapter as a phenomenological frame of reference for conceiving experientially how literary metaphor presentationally amplifies poetic and narrative themes.

The opening section of chapter 3 focuses on theories of the literary image. After offering a critique of Theodore Ziolkowski's view of the literary image as icon, I argue that such imagery is more fundamentally constitutive of human awareness than Ziolkowski contends, that it is in fact a *symbolic form*, and that literary images communicate by means of descriptions and depictions. Section 2 illustrates this conception of the nature and efficacy of the literary image by applying it practically in an analysis of narrative imagery in Henry James's *The Golden Bowl*. Appealing directly to literary experience, rather than to theoretical contexts of meaning extrinsic to the narrative, this section of chapter 3 shows how James's literary images—extended metaphors, really—*depictively* further the characterization of Adam Verver and dramatically realize the evolution of Maggie Verver's consciousness of the liaison between her husband, Amerigo, and Charlotte Stant, her stepmother. Following the discussion and illustration in sections 1 and 2 of the depictive function in literary imagery, section 3 defines depiction as it operates within the context of literary experience. Depictive literary imagery is posited as articulating perceived relationships (between objects, people, ideas, or feelings) in a presentationally immediate form that permits the literary reader to assimilate them "whole," as it were, with perceptual immediacy, and with all the vivacity of their dramatic impact—which is the experiential index of their narrative efficacy.

In order to clarify further the depictive view of literary metaphor, section 4 considers two phenomenological approaches to metaphor that in different ways anticipate the theory introduced in the present work. Although I find it problematic on a number of counts, Marcus B. Hester's *Meaning of Poetic Metaphor* adumbrates the depictive view outlined in the present work by stressing the primacy of the presentational quality of metaphoric imagery. And George E. Yoos's seminal, if frequently neglected, "Phenomenological Look at Metaphor" acutely delineates the presuppositions and limits of analytic, as opposed to experiential, theories of metaphor. By way of conclusion, section 5 inquires into the understanding of literary metaphor. After recapitulating main points of the approach to depictive imagery and literary experience developed through chapters 2 and 3, this final section probes the implications of explicating literary metaphor from the perspectives of two diverse universes of discourse: that of abstract or formal analysis and that of phenomenological awareness. The study of metaphor and literary experience essayed here closes with a brief explication of a key metaphor in Emily Dickinson's vivid "A Bird Came Down the

Walk," an image considered in the opening section of the first chapter in the context of appraising Aristotelian theories.

It should become clear in what follows that I do not pretend to put forward any definitive formula or privileged heuristic for interpreting literary metaphor. I do hope, however, to clarify how metaphor communicates meaning and thereby enriches literary experience.

CHAPTER ONE

Metaphor

PROMINENT VIEWS
AND CRITICAL ASSESSMENTS

A better understanding of metaphor is one of the aims which an
improved curriculum of literary study might well set before itself.

I . A . R I C H A R D S
Practical Criticism

1. Aristotelian Approaches

The epistemological presuppositions—the assumptions about how things
can be known—that underlie the pioneering studies in any realm of
experience generally not only determine the focus and the direction of
subsequent inquiry but also go far toward establishing the criteria of formal
discourse on a topic. [1] The Cartesian mind-body duality in philosophy and
the psychological phenomenon of transference posited by Freud are two
notable examples of such foundational epistemological assumptions. In
the study of metaphor, deductive analysis, essentially the "dividing and
collecting in accordance with kinds" (as philosopher Stanley Rosen translates the Greek *diaeresis*), [2] is the strategy of explanation, indeed the
fundamental assumption of how in principle we come to know, that Aristotle employs in his seminal definitions of metaphor[3] in the *Poetics* (1457b)
and in the *Rhetoric* (1406b, 1410b, 1412a). [4]

Although he cites literary examples, Aristotle's observations on metaphor are not developed in light of any comprehensive theory of literary
experience. The scattered explanations of metaphor that occur in Aris-

totle's writings, although suggestive, are not in fact part of any sustained and cogent analysis. In his well-known *Greek Metaphor*,[5] W. B. Stanford concludes that in Aristotle's discussions in the *Poetics* and in the *Rhetoric* metaphor

> fails to receive the systematic and exhaustive treatment accorded to a major subject like Metaphysics. So whereas in Logic or Politics or in any of his main theses Aristotle makes an admirable leader, in Metaphor it is pitiful to observe how his followers are blind to the inadequacies and imperfections of his treatment; how where Aristotle's classifications of Metaphor are too rigid or abstract, his examples unsystematic and careless, his analysis biassed and incomplete, yet every detail of his misjudgment is applauded and exaggerated by his disciples. (P. 5)

Although the tone is somewhat less than objective and the passage dates from 1936, Stanford's statement remains substantially accurate despite the avalanche of studies on metaphor published over the last half-century.

In more recent assessments, philosopher Mark Johnson and semiologist Umberto Eco (see note 3) each find that most theorists of metaphor are still fundamentally disciples of Aristotle. In his introduction to *Philosophical Perspectives on Metaphor*, Johnson identifies a highly influential Aristotelian "triad of half-truths" that informs contemporary views of the metaphoric process: the

> (i) focus on single words that are (ii) deviations from literal language, to produce a change of meaning that is (iii) based on similarities between things. (P. 6)

Citing the *Rhetoric* (1406b), Johnson indicates a fourth problematic point in Aristotle's approach to metaphor in the dictum that metaphor is an elliptical simile.

Such is the influence of Aristotle's pronouncements, however, that even putatively non-Aristotelian theories rarely avoid presupposing Aristotelian notions. In *Metaphor Reexamined: A Non-Aristotelian Perspective*, for instance, Liselotte Gumpel attempts to supersede Aristotelian theories by concentrating on "broad meaning before idiosyncratic metaphor, function before form, and holistic context before taxonomy" (p. xii). An elaborate (and jargon-laden)[6] synthesis of Peircean semiotics and the phenomenological semantics of Roman Ingarden, Gumpel's theory relies ultimately on the unanalyzed Aristotelian concept of *transfer*[7] as the operative principle in metaphor. As she puts it,

Transference . . . causes selected constituents [of a metaphorical expression's "literal" sense] to *shift* in their reference in order to release authorial intent as new, unified meaning. . . . The chosen explicit denominations constitute "reference," while the implicit ones arise with transference in new semantic integration. That is the processing "natural" to a natural language. (P. 54)

In addition to the idea of transfer upon which theorists such as Gumpel construct their theory, three other abstract and unanalyzed primitives appear in Aristotle's explanations of metaphor: comparison, substitution, and analogy.[8] When applied in practical criticism, all four of these concepts prove inadequate as explanations of the mechanism of metaphor, something that I aim in this section to illustrate. It is first necessary, however, to be clear as to what theories predicated on each of the four Aristotelian primitives assume about how metaphor operates.

Max Black in *Models and Metaphors* defines the substitution theory, which he asserts is the most general of the Aristotelian perspectives,[9] as "any view which holds that a metaphorical expression is used in place of some equivalent expression" (p. 31). Although in Black's opinion substitution theories are those that identify metaphorical meaning with literal paraphrase (such that a figurative term is held to be replaceable by an appropriate literal term without any sacrifice of cognitive content), practically every theory of metaphor that differentiates between the literal and the figurative signification of expressions recognized as metaphorical is in some sense a substitution view.[10] Substitution theories presuppose the identity or underlying resemblance between the extension of a metaphorical term and that for which it "substitutes." They regard metaphor as an indirect means of conveying some underlying literal meaning. According to substitution views, metaphor is a play of equivalent terms that, while actuated by perception of resemblance between things, is essentially an instance of interchanging words and phrases in suitable contexts. The distinguishing factor among substitution theories is their explanation of the character of the metaphorical "equivalence" between correlative figurative and literal terms (such as between "bull" and "John" in "John is a bull") and their views on the mechanism of substitution (a primitive intuitive act, for instance, or a semantic transfer of some sort).

Alternatively, metaphor is still commonly understood and taught as Aristotle defined it in the *Rhetoric* (1410b): "an elliptical simile, a *comparison* of things without the use of 'like' or 'as.' " Comparison theories typically rely upon the notion of transfer in accounting for the operation of

metaphor, although they do not necessarily posit the perception of resemblance between literal and figurative meanings as essential to the
making of metaphor. Comparison views that do not assert the perception of
similarity between literal and figurative terms constitute a subcategory of
the substitution approach, one for which the idea of semantic "transference" often serves as the mechanism of substitution. For example, in
Black's by now tired example, "Man is a wolf," a comparison theorist
would hold that "wolf" operates metaphorically through a transfer of
meanings, such as wild and predatory, from the literal extension of the
word to "Man"—a transfer that is consequent upon a comparison between
the two terms as they occur in the context of the sentence.[11]

Analogy theories presuppose comparison and transfer, although in a
somewhat restricted sense. Paul Henle articulates the general principles
of the analogy view when he states that

> metaphor, as distinguished from other tropes, depends on analogy, and in this
> analogy one side is used to represent the other. . . . In each case we are led to think
> of something by a consideration of something like it. (In Johnson, p. 87)

Analogies involve comparisons, although comparisons are not restricted to
the search for analogies. (The perception of disanalogies might well be the
cause, method, or goal of a given comparison.) To compare is thus not
necessarily to analogize; on the other hand, every analogy implies a
comparison of two items, one of which, in metaphor, is substituted for
("represents") the other by a transfer of the salient meanings of the
figurative term to the context of the word or phrase for which it substitutes.[12] In the sentence, "Old age is the evening of life," for example,
the comparison between "old age" and "life" is based, according to
Aristotle, on the perception of the following analogy, succinctly rendered
by Warren Shibles in his *Analysis of Metaphor:* "If old age : life : : evening
: day, then we may speak of evening as the 'old age of the day,' and 'old
age' as the 'evening of life' " (p. 118).[13] The sense of what "evening"
represents (that for which it could be said to substitute) is attributable on
this account of metaphor to the transfer of suitable meaning from all that
"evening" *could* connote to just what it *should* connote in context, a
transfer predicated on analogues between "life" and "day."

In the teaching of literature the value of a metaphoric concept—say,
that literary metaphor is fundamentally a transfer of meaning from a word's
literal to its figurative signification—inheres, clearly enough, in its practi-

cability. It is to practical criticism, then, that we turn to determine the implications, and hence in William James's phrase the "cash value," of the Aristotelian theories of comparison, transfer, substitution, and analogy in construing *how* a metaphor means.

In connection with literary metaphor, Benjamin Hrushovski makes the pertinent point (one that I stressed in the introduction) that

> many of the prominent studies [of metaphor] have come from disciplines outside of literary criticism such as philosophy, psychology, linguistics, which are usually more oriented toward rational theoretical analysis. ("Poetic Metaphor and Frames of Reference," p. 5)

Walker Percy discerns a problematic dichotomy (one the present study aims to avoid) between literary and philosophical approaches in the conceptualization of metaphor:

> The difficulty has been that inquiries into the nature of metaphor have tended to be either literary or philosophical with neither side having much use for the other. The subject is divided into its formal and material aspects, with philosophers trying to arrive at the nature of metaphor by abstracting from all metaphors, beautiful and commonplace, and with critics paying attention to the particular devices by which a poet brings off his effects. ("Metaphors as Mistake," pp. 66–67)

With a phenomenon as ubiquitous and fundamental to literary experience as metaphor, detailed explications of literary metaphor based on the working assumptions of disciplines not concerned in the first instance with literature can hardly avoid reductive formulations.

Considering in Aristotelian terms how the metaphor *swim* operates in the Emily Dickinson poem that follows will help determine in a practical context whether and to what degree comparison, transfer, substitution, and analogy are abstract or reductive labels that fail to make coherent literary sense of a poetic metaphor.

> A Bird came down the Walk—
> He did not know I saw—
> He bit an Angleworm in halves
> And ate the fellow, raw,
>
> And then he drank a Dew
> From a convenient Grass—
> And then hopped sidewise to the Wall
> To let a Beetle pass—

He glanced with rapid eyes
That hurried all around—
They looked like frightened Beads, I thought—
He stirred his Velvet Head

Like one in danger, Cautious,
I offered him a Crumb
And he unrolled his feathers
And rowed him softer home—

Than Oars divide the Ocean,
Too silver for a seam—
Or Butterflies, off Banks of Noon
Leap, plashless as they swim.

                                    (*Complete Poems*, p. 156)

From an Aristotelian perspective, the verb *swim* is a semantic deviation, a deliberate misnomer, since it normally characterizes an activity quite different from what butterflies do when they leap "off Banks / of Noon." An effect of this poetical misnaming is that it elicits a comparison, as would simile, of two diverse sorts of actions—swimming and flying.[14] Yet unlike simile, the metaphor can be regarded as a comparison that actually applies, attributes, or transfers notions associated with swimming directly to the image of butterflies in flight.[15] A comparison of any sort presupposes a basis of similarity, identity,[16] or a "common feature."[17] Conceived as comparison, the metaphorical functioning of swim could be expected to reveal some formerly unperceived similarities[18] (either directly or by means of analogy) between swimming and flight as they relate to the bird's movement in the context of the poem. Or the metaphor *swim* might, in the words of philosopher Karsten Harries, "create something altogether new."[19]

Interpreting swim on the word-level,[20] however, fails to account for how the concept of *to swim* functions metaphorically in the poem, if we attend to the poem as a whole instead of merely to the metaphor as the operative term of a preconceived formula or process. How, for instance, does the substitution (regardless of the way it is effected) of any of the literal referents of swim in characterizing flight explain the metaphor's function of slowing the pace of the motion depicted in the poem? This difficulty indicates the imperative of accounting for the vivid drama that develops through five preceding stanzas, not focusing just on the possible senses of the metaphorical term. If swim is metaphorical exclusively as, or as the result of, a comparison of some sort, comprehending Dickinson's poem would amount to an activity of conscious analysis, a riddle-solving game involving the deliberative evaluation of similarities, differences, or some unique aspect of swimming or flight. Conceiving the verse poetically, however, in the context, that is, of literary experience, means apprehending swim prediscursively,[21] as a component of an integrated field of meaning: as part of the "world"[22] of the poem.

The metaphors of literary experience are grounded, in the first instance, in a thematic—not a linguistic or semiotic—matrix. In literature themes are the ways in which ideas and events are made significant, made expressive of meaning that transcends discrete boundaries between thoughts and happenings by integrating them into an aesthetic whole. Literary themes articulate the most nuanced of thoughts and feelings, communicating them with sensuous immediacy through their presentational rendering—their dramatization—as narrative events. (Walter J. Ong has gone so far as to assert that "Without themes, there would be no way to deal with events.")[23] Literary art aspires toward communicating human events—physical, social, and those of consciousness—with all the prereflective impact of drama, that is, in a manner unmediated by trains of discursive thought; and the depiction of themes in the imagery of metaphor, explained in detail in chapter 2 and in the third section of chapter 3, is the way that with dramatic immediacy literary artists assimilate and thereby enrich particular events with the themes of our common experience. By dramatizing events of awareness and of action imagistically, metaphors both express and amplify the themes that occasion them.

The less richly articulated the thematic context of a literary metaphor, the more indeterminate and trivial is its meaning—a trivial live metaphor can mean virtually almost anything and so has virtually no presentational definition, no dramatic character. Unfortunately, free-floating metaphors like "wolf" in Black's example frequently serve as paradigms in analyses of how metaphor operates. As Hrushovski pertinently suggests, "It is not clear that theory developed in light of trivial instances of metaphor is transferable to more extensive and obscure instances of creative metaphors" ("Poetic Metaphor," p. 6).

Basing inquiries into how metaphors mean on examples grounded in minimal or indeterminate thematic contexts leads, in the case of literary metaphor, to the neglect or underestimation of the seminal role thematic development plays in the realization of metaphorical meaning. [24] A consequence is the formulation of theories, such as those based on the act of comparing, that when practically applied to literary experience yield distorted or incomplete accounts of how metaphor operates. Analyses of literary metaphor based on the comparison approach typically focus construal of meaning on the level of the word rather than on that of the sentence or of a complete unit of discourse. In doing so they mistake *a reading* for *reading* and tacitly assume that literary experience is a series of discrete instances of discursive, comparative analysis, rather than a processive, integrally unified, dramatically evolved apprehension. [25]

To be sure, critics take exception to the comparison theory on other grounds as well. And since this approach to metaphor has been, as Johnson notes, "the single most popular and widespread account of how metaphors work" (*Philosophical Perspectives*, p. 25), it is worthwhile to consider some of the fundamental challenges to it posed by leading critics, challenges incidentally that apply by and large to all Aristotelian theories of metaphor. In his critical summary of the history of speculation about metaphor, Johnson touches on five telling objections to the comparison theory. For the first objection he refers to Black's classic 1954 essay on the topic, recounting Black's charge that comparison views do not

> tell us how we are to compute the meaning of any given metaphor. Any two objects are similar in some respects and the comparison view does not explain how we are able to pick out the relevant similarities in each instance. (*Philosophical Perspectives*, p. 26)

As Black himself put it:

> The main objection against a comparison view is that it suffers from vagueness that borders upon vacuity. We are supposed to be puzzled as to how some expression (M), used metaphorically, can function in place of some literal expression (L) that is held to be an approximate synonym, and the answer offered is that what M stands for (in its literal use) is *similar* to what L stands for. But how informative is this? . . . Metaphorical statement is not a substitute for a formal comparison or any other kind of literal statement, but has its own distinctive capacities and achievements. (*Models and Metaphors*, p. 37)

The second objection to the comparison theory that Johnson cites is an argument first made by I. A. Richards in his groundbreaking analysis of metaphor in the fifth chapter of *The Philosophy of Rhetoric:*

by overemphasizing the role of similarities, the theory ignores the sometimes crucial role of differences and disanalogies. The insight we gain is often less a product of perceived similarities highlighted by the metaphor and more a result of dissimilarities that force us imaginatively to restructure our way of comprehending things.[26]

For the third, fourth, and fifth charges against comparison theories of metaphor, Johnson relies mainly on the discussion of metaphor in John Searle's *Expression and Meaning*.[27] The first objection is that frequently metaphor does not refer to two *actual* things that can be compared. This notorious couplet from Milton's "Lycidas" is an example:

> But that two-handed engine at the door,
> Stands ready to smite once, and smite no more.
> (*Complete Poems*, p. 124)

According to Merritt Y. Hughes (whose *reading*, not the validity of his analysis, is of interest here), "two-handed" refers to the two Houses of Parliament and "engine" is "a symbol of its power to establish true liberty" (in Elledge, p. 296). The power to establish anything, insofar as it is mere potential, is not in itself an actual object for comparison. Samuel R. Levin, for one, would dispute this assertion. In "Standard Approaches to Metaphor and a Proposal for Literary Metaphor," he takes issue with this objection of Searle's, arguing that the comparison theory does not require that the objects compared actually exist.[28]

Searle's second objection is that relevant statements of similarity between the things compared may be false, as when the characteristics associated with the literal meaning of a term are not true to the facts. A notable instance of this occurs in Tennyson's "Locksley Hall." As the poet's biographer Robert Bernard Martin explains,

> Tennyson used to tell how they had arrived in Liverpool in time to take the first train that ever ran between that city and Manchester, on 20 September. . . . In their hurry to get aboard the crowded train they were unable to see the wheels because of the press of spectators on the platform, and the near-sighted Tennyson could not see them after in the dark, so that he assumed they were running in grooves. The result of his myopia was a line composed that night which became one of his most famous when it was ultimately embedded in "Locksley Hall": "Let the great world spin for ever down the ringing grooves of change." (*Tennyson*, p. 191)

Searle's position that comparison theories do not adequately elucidate metaphor because of the possible failure of an image to conform, in its literal sense, to reality is a correlate of his first criticism. Searle bases both objections on the assumption that comparison theories involve the comparison of things as they actually are, and Levin's counterclaim obtains in both instances.

The third point Searle makes against the comparison approach to metaphor is that "for many metaphors there simply are not literal similarities between objects as required by the theory" (in Johnson, p. 27). An instance of such a metaphor appears in this wonderfully comic stanza from a poem by Dickinson:

> The Hopes so juicy ripening—
> You almost bathed your Tongue—
> When Bliss disclosed a hundred Toes—
> And fled with every one—
> *(Complete Poems*, p. 247)

The literal expression of "a hundred Toes" has no bearing on "Bliss," except in some metaphorical sense. And a theory of metaphor that relies on a comparison of this sort does not explain a thing, for it relies on circular reasoning (the meaning of the metaphor being its metaphorical sense).

Johnson summarizes the criticism of the comparison approach by concluding that theorists who subscribe to comparison views "make at least two mistakes":

> First, they assume that because similarity often plays a role in our comprehension of a metaphor, it is therefore the essence of the *meaning* of the metaphor; and, second, they take similarity as the sole basis for the act of comprehension. (*Philosophical Perspectives*, p. 27)

In "More About Metaphor," written twenty-two years after his earlier piece on the topic, Black takes the comparison view to task on grounds that extend the line of criticism Johnson adduces (although Johnson's historical introduction appeared four years later, in 1981). Black claims that to assume that a metaphorical statement

> is an abstract or precis of a literal point-by-point comparison, in which the primary and secondary subjects are juxtaposed for the sake of noting dissimilarities as well as similarities, is to misconstrue the function of metaphor. In discursively comparing one subject *with* another, we sacrifice the distinctive power and effectiveness of a

good metaphor. The literal comparison lacks the ambience and suggestiveness, and the imposed "view" of the primary subject, upon which a metaphor's power to illuminate depends. (In Ortony, p. 32)

In "The Metaphorical Twist" (1962), Monroe Beardsley had earlier voiced a related criticism, citing the deficiency of comparison theories of metaphor in the context of literary interpretation:

> Once we commit ourselves to finding or supplying an object to be compared with the subject of the metaphor (that is, in I. A. Richards's terms, a "vehicle" to make it go) we open the way for that flow of idiosyncratic imagery that is one of the serious barriers between a reader and a poem. (In Johnson, p. 107)

Beardsley's position is that the comparison approach (and by implication theories claiming metaphor to be a function of substitution, semantic transfer, or analogy) affords no determinate way of fixing the imagery metaphor elicits vis-à-vis a given "tenor" in such a way that the imagery could enlighten a reader about the meaning of a poem. He concludes that a comparison theory "tempts the explicator to invent, where he cannot discover a 'vehicle' " (in Johnson, p. 108).

Considering the inadequacy of the comparison theory from a different angle, Searle astutely points, in a critique that is more telling than those of his that Johnson cites, to an inherent confusion over whether the "comparing" is itself a *component* of metaphorical meaning or merely a *process that facilitates it:*

> One might say the endemic vice of the comparison theories is that they fail to distinguish between the claim that the statement of the comparison is part of the *meaning,* and hence the *truth conditions,* of the metaphorical statement, and the claim that the statement of the similarity is the *principle of inference,* or a step in the process of *comprehending,* on the basis of which speakers produce and hearers understand metaphor. (In Ortony, p. 100)

In a "phenomenological description of our apprehension of metaphor,"[29] George E. Yoos calls the comparison view to account on experiential grounds:

> There is no *necessary* awareness of analogy, likeness, or comparison when we conceive of one object, quality, or action through the form of another. ("A Phenomenological Look at Metaphor," p. 84)

Charles O. Hartman offers still other grounds for dismissing the comparison perspective when, referring to a metaphor that identifies a woman with a guitar, he declares that

> comparison with things we know allows us to comprehend what we do not. Metaphors sometimes do this; but I know as well what a guitar is and what a woman is, before I compare them as after. ("Cognitive Metaphor," p. 329)

Hartman thus contends—and all who challenge the comparison approach would concur—that it is not plausible to conceive the power of a metaphor to communicate fresh insights in terms of the act of comparison.

In the face of criticism such as the foregoing, it is clear that as suggestive as some aspects of Aristotelian theories of metaphor are, they fail to provide a satisfactory account of how literary metaphors operate.

2. *Interaction Theories*

What is generally recognized as the first significant break in this century with Aristotelian theory in the study of metaphor appeared in 1936, the same year that Stanford's analysis and critique of Aristotle's views was published. In the fifth lecture of *The Philosophy of Rhetoric*, I. A. Richards details what, eighteen years later, Max Black was to christen the "interaction view."[30] Essentially a radical alternative to explanations of metaphor that look to comparison, substitution, transfer, or analogy, the interaction theory posits the operation of metaphor as primarily a cognitive process, not a linguistic or semiotic one (not, as Richards put it, a "verbal matter") that words merely "support."[31] From this perspective, the actuating moment of metaphorical meaning is an interaction of thoughts. In place of notions of equivalence, resemblance, or transfer, interaction approaches stress a fundamentally different transformational function of metaphorical expressions in their semantic context.

Defining the operation of metaphor as the "interaction of two copresent thoughts," Richards asserts that

> In the simplest formulation, when we use a metaphor we have two thoughts of different things active together and supported by a single word, or phrase, whose meaning is a resultant of their interaction. (*Philosophy of Rhetoric*, p. 93)

In this discussion Richards introduces what have since become standard descriptive terms, *tenor* and *vehicle*, to denote respectively the principal subject and figurative term of a metaphorical expression.

A brief look at the practical applicability of Richards's theory will clarify the strengths and limitations of his highly influential anatomy of metaphor. Consider the metaphor "cliff / Of Norway" in the fourth stanza of Allen Tate's moving "Death of Little Boys":

Death of Little Boys

When little boys grow patient at last, weary,
Surrender their eyes immeasurably to the night,
The event will rage terrific as the sea;
Their bodies fill a crumbling room with light.

Then you will touch at the bedside, torn in two,
Gold curls now deftly intricate with gray
As the windowpane extends a fear to you
From one peeled aster drenched with the wind all day.

And over his chest the covers, in an ultimate dream,
Will mount to the teeth, ascend the eyes, press back
The locks—while round his sturdy belly gleam
The suspended breaths, white spars above the wreck:

Till all the guests, come in to look, turn down
Their palms; and delirium assails the cliff
Of Norway where you ponder, and your little town
Reels like a sailor drunk in his rotten skiff. . . .

The bleak sunshine shrieks its chipped music then
Out to the milkweed amid the fields of wheat.
There is a calm for you where men and women
Unroll the chill precision of moving feet.

(Poems, p. 3)

According to Richards's view, the thought of a "cliff / Of Norway" as a metaphoric vehicle "cooperates" with the conception of the poem's mournful tenor (in the sense of a "borrowing between" or "intercourse") to effect some "inclusive meaning" (*Philosophy of Rhetoric,* p. 119). More specifically, "cliff / Of Norway" is to be understood as controlling in a unique way "the mode in which the tenor [the parent's grief] forms" (p. 122). This would seem to indicate that the image somehow contributes to thematic development. The apprehension of the image as metaphor is the entertainment of "two thoughts of different things *active together* and supported by a single word or phrase, whose meaning is a resultant of their interaction" (p. 122).

Although Richards's concept of interaction is somewhat vague, "cliff / Of Norway" can be conceived as deriving and conveying its metaphorical sense from two thoughts that in some way interact—one thought of a geographical location (a cliff) and the other of an emotional state (of a consciousness rendered delirious through overwhelming grief). Despite a certain lack of conceptual rigor—Exactly how do the thoughts interact? In what way are they "active together"?—Richards's formulation was revolutionary in the history of speculation about metaphor, and it inspired Black's more closely reasoned effort at working out a credible version of the interaction account.

Like Richards, Black considers metaphor a "double unit" composed of a semantic setting and an image, a "frame" and a "focus." Insofar as the notion of frame is more determinately suggestive than Richards's tenor, however, Black is clearer than his predecessor on the role of context in metaphorical meaning. Black finds Richards's theory original and compelling, yet he is careful to note the use of metaphor in the very formulation of the interaction approach to metaphor:

> To speak of the "interaction" of two thoughts "active together" (or again, of their "interillumination" or "cooperation") is to *use* a metaphor emphasizing the dynamic aspects of a good reader's response to a nontrivial metaphor. (*Models and Metaphors*, p. 39)

To explicate the dynamics of a "good" reader's comprehension of nontrivial metaphor, Black elaborates on his conception of *focus*, explaining it as a filter through which a "system of commonplaces" or in "suitable cases . . . deviant implications [of the figurative term] established *ad hoc* by the writer" are somehow screened. The "focusing" that Black asserts metaphorical terms effect in some way rearranges perception of the "principal subject," or "frame."[32] The modification of awareness occurs through a process of selection, emphasis, suppression, and organization of "features of the principal subject by implying (or 'projecting upon' it) statements about it that normally apply to the subsidiary subject [the meaning of the figurative expression outside of any metaphorical context]" (p. 44).

In "More about Metaphor" (1977), Black revises some of his terminology (renaming "principal subject" the "primary subject" and changing "subsidiary subject" to "secondary subject"), dropping as "needlessly paradoxical, though not plainly mistaken" the contention that primary subjects are "often best regarded as '*systems* of things' rather than 'things.' " In addition, he reconceives the notion of the "system of associated commonplaces" (something predicable of the secondary subject and metaphorically "projected" onto the frame, the primary subject) as a "set of associated implications" or "implicative complex."[33] In an extended amplification of his views, Black concisely articulates the essence of his interactionist approach to metaphor by explaining what he means in asserting that in metaphor two "subjects" interact:

> (a) the presence of the primary subject incites the hearer to select some of the secondary subject's properties; and (b) invites him to construct a parallel implication-complex that can fit the primary subject; and (c) reciprocally induces parallel changes in the secondary subject. (In Ortony, p. 24)

To assess the practicability of Black's theory, consider once again "cliff / Of Norway" in "Death of Little Boys." If we follow Black, comprehending how the metaphor operates presumably involves first determining the primary subject—the progress of the parent's grief over the dead child. The mere presence of the subject (Black remains unclear as to whether the subject is to be conceived as a "system")[34] "incites" the selection of "some of the secondary subject's properties" (in Ortony, p. 29). Precisely how this poem's deeply affecting depiction of a devastating emotional experience "invites" the reader to undertake, and then governs, a process of selection from among the properties of the "cliff / Of Norway" remains on Black's account uncertain. Further, to characterize the uniquely rendered experience of bereavement generically, as a "subject," for purposes of clarifying how the metaphor operates, is reductive; it provides no reason for doubting why any occurrence of the identical primary subject—regardless of language, say, or of idiom—should not occasion the identical metaphor. In other words, what is unique about the poem is factored out. Also problematic is how the reader is invited (after the process of selection) to "construct [in some undisclosed way] a parallel implication-complex," one that will somehow "fit the primary subject." What Black intends by the terms *parallel* and *fit* remains obscure and indeed sounds a lot like standard comparison theory strategies that, to quote again part of Beardsley's criticism, "open the way for that flow of idiosyncratic imagery that is one of the serious barriers between a reader and a poem" (in Johnson, p. 107).

Black maintains that the resulting "fitting" of diversely originating implication-complexes that occurs in the reader's act of reading "reciprocally induces parallel changes" in the "primary subject" and in "cliff / Of Norway." According to Black, then, the interaction of "cliff / Of Norway" is the stimulation of reciprocal parallel changes in two subjects, changes determined by mutually relevant implication-complexes. More specifically, the metaphor operates through the reader's projecting or fitting images of solitude, starkness, windiness, and bleakness—all related implications readily associated with the secondary subject—onto the frame (the experience of parental grief as it is narratively developed through the poem) which those images amplify by means of some unexplained aspect of the interaction. At the same time, the implications associated with the figurative term undergo thematically germane amplification themselves—solitude, for instance, takes on the sense of forlornness. We might summarize Black's approach by citing his assertion that, "We can say that the principal subject is 'seen through' the metaphorical expression" (*Models and Metaphors*, p. 41).

In taking account of the primacy of semantic context in explaining metaphorical meaning—by understanding, that is, the primary subject as a metaphor's frame—Black's interaction theory (and to a lesser degree Richards's) more nearly reflects the way metaphor operates in literary experience than do comparison views that posit metaphorical meaning as a result of readers comprehending the signification of figurative terms that function as discrete units of meaning. His contention, however, that metaphor is at bottom an operation of "applying" or "projecting" or "fitting" of implicative complexes is an abstract and clumsy structural expedient that betrays the analytical positivism typical of most of the theoretical approaches to metaphor since Aristotle. In practice, Black's view ignores the unified "thematic" or narrative flow—what Northrop Frye (borrowing from Aristotle) terms the *mythos*[35]—that constitutes the ground of literary comprehension and the idiom of literary experience. Nor does Black's theory explain how the image of the "cliff / Of Norway" assimilates freely, is "naturalized" as it were, into the poetic narrative—how it *becomes* the language, the *logos*, of the poem.

As with the comparison theories of metaphor, Black's version of "interactionism" has been taken to task on a variety of counts. Although he considers his approach to metaphor more cogent than others, Black himself expresses dissatisfaction with it even after the modifications and developments made over the years since he first introduced it in the mid-fifties. In 1978, he confessed that the interaction theory is deficient in its "lack of clarification of what it means to say that in metaphor one thing is thought of (or viewed) *as* another thing" (in Sacks, p. 192). It is difficult to think of a more fundamental criticism of Black's approach.

George Yoos discerns a misstep in both Black's and Richards's accounts where "the attention turns from thoughts to words in their analyses of metaphor. . . . in so doing they turn from the question of what metaphor is like descriptively to the question of what we are doing in the name of interpretation" ("A Phenomenological Look at Metaphor," p. 83).

John Searle, whose distinction between a speaker's meaning and the meaning of a speaker's utterance is the basis of a suggestive though incomplete[36] two-stage approach to metaphor (one that has affinities with Beardsley's "verbal-opposition" theory, which I take up in the next section), concludes that "semantic interaction theories were developed in response to the weakness of the comparison theories," and states that he has "never seen any convincing examples, nor even halfway clear account of what 'interaction' is supposed to mean" (in Ortony, p. 119). Focusing on the two semantic categories of interaction views, Searle finds

> an endemic failure to appreciate the distinction between sentence or word meaning, which is never metaphorical, and speaker or utterance meaning, which can be metaphorical.[37]

In a comment that substantiates objections raised against Black's theory in connection with the metaphor from Tate's poem, Searle notes that

> proponents of the interaction view see correctly that the mental processes and the semantic processes involved in producing and understanding metaphorical utterances cannot involve references themselves, but must be at the level of intentionality, that is they must involve relations at the level of beliefs, meanings, associations, and so on. However, they then say incorrectly that the relations in question must be some unexplained, but metaphorically described, relations of "interaction" between a literal frame and a metaphorical focus.[38]

Michael Polanyi and Harry Prosch argue in "From Perception to Metaphor" that, "at best," Black's theory

> shows only that we can learn something from a metaphor that we did not know before and that this has something to do with a "suitable" reader's capacity to make a connection between "the two ideas" in a metaphor. (In *Meaning*, p. 76)

Finally, Israel Scheffler finds "the appeal to unexplained meaning changes in Black's account of metaphor a serious limitation" (*Beyond the Letter*, p. 112). The problem, to recur to Tate's poem, of how the peculiar bleakness of a cliff of Norway is to be projected nonmetaphorically onto, and thus amplify the meaning of, the primary subject of "Death of Little Boys," remains unresolved.

3. *Controversion, Verbal-Opposition, Iconic Signification, and Supervenience (Intuitionism) Theories*

Since the appearance of Black's interaction theory, a host of alternative ways of thinking about metaphor have been published. Four of the most original and influential are the controversion, verbal-opposition, iconic signification, and supervenience theories. A brief, critical appraisal of each of these approaches suggests how developments in the history of the idea of metaphor have evolved in the direction of the experiential view that I introduce in chapter 3.

As Warren Shibles explains in his *Analysis of Metaphor*, controversion accounts of metaphor conceive a

> metaphorical statement [as] a statement which is logically (or literally) absurd. Therefore the metaphor must be understood in a way which makes the metaphorical sentence non-literal yet meaningful. (Pp. 66–67)

Controversion views, like interaction theories, focus on the transformational function of expressions that are metaphorical. From this perspective, recognizing the logical absurdity of the figurative expression that occurs in place of (substitutes for) a literal expression triggers the apprehension of metaphorical meaning. Like substitution views, controversion theories posit the actuating moment of metaphor in the play of denotative, or literal, word sense. Controversion views thus straddle substitution and interaction perspectives.

Beardsley's verbal-opposition theory is perhaps the most frequently discussed version of the controversion approach. It details with some plausibility the manifestation of metaphorical meaning as a function of the recognition of logical absurdity. According to Beardsley,

> a metaphorical attribution . . . involves two ingredients: a semantic distinction between two levels of meaning, and a logical opposition on one level. . . . it describes the shift [or "twist" as he termed it in the later version of his theory] from designation to connotation. (In Johnson, p. 112)

In his revised theory Beardsley explains that a figurative expression's connotations that are unusual or that may be unique to its occurrence in, say, a particular poem—connotations that are context-specific—are distinguished from familiar or "staple connotations," by being "drawn from the *total* set of accidental properties either found in or attributed to such objects" (emphasis added).

To apply Beardsley's approach to a familiar example, consider again the metaphor *swim* from the Dickinson poem discussed in the opening section of the present chapter. The two "levels" of meaning that are presumably ingredients in the apprehension of the verb as metaphor would be (1) that of the overt actions being poeticized: the flight of a bird and the flight of butterflies to which it is compared; and (2) that attaching to swim. The "logical opposition" would pertain to the second level: swimming stands opposed to flight. A difficulty with the theory to note here is that the opposition actually involves *both* levels equally. Indeed, it could not take place on just one level: what would oppose swim? At any rate, Beardsley explains that the logical opposition

> includes both direct incompatibility of designated properties and a more indirect incompatibility between the presuppositions of the terms—as when our concept of the sun rules out the possibility of voluntary behavior that is presupposed [in the expression "the spiteful sun"] by the term "spiteful." (In Johnson, p. 112)

In Beardsley's view, this opposition "describes the shift" in the sense of what, for instance, *swim* in the Dickinson example signifies from denotations to connotations apropos its context in the poem. Consequent upon the perception of verbal opposition, then, the figurative verb with which Dickinson's poem concludes is recognized, in Beardsley's account, not as indicative of the action of a living being propelling itself through a liquid medium but as suggestive of some set of connotations of swim that apply to the flight of butterflies as compared to the flight of a bird.

As one might expect, the notion of "verbal opposition" has drawn its share of critical fire. Black, for instance, objects on the grounds that it is not unique to metaphor:

> this test, so far as it fits, will apply equally to such other tropes as oxymoron or hyperbole [Paul Ricoeur in *The Rule of Metaphor* cites irony (pp. 94–95)], so that it would at best certify the presence of some figurative statement, but not necessarily metaphor. (In Ortony, p. 35)

Black cites a more fundamental weakness of the controversion approach
when he declares that

> authentic metaphors need not manifest the invoked controversion. . . . The negation
> of any metaphorical statement can itself be a metaphorical statement and hence
> possibly true if taken literally. (In Ortony, p. 35)

By way of illustration, Black offers the following example: "Man is not
a wolf but an ostrich." Though true literally, the clause "Man is not a
wolf" is, in the context of the sentence, "as metaphorical as its opposite,
yet it clearly fails the controversion test [i.e., logical opposition]" (in
Ortony, p. 35).

Paul Ricoeur raises doubts about Beardsley's concept of the "potential
range of connotation" as the reservoir of meaning that permits an expression to operate as metaphor. He asks rhetorically whether newly invented
metaphors are not "just those metaphors that add to this storehouse of
commonplaces, this range of connotations?" (*The Rule of Metaphor*,
p. 97). If, for instance, swim as it occurs in the context of the Dickinson
poem takes on unfamiliar connotations, such as the grace of movement of
butterflies' wings, how can those connotations be understood to explain the
way that swim operates as metaphor when the image takes on those connotations precisely *because* it operates metaphorically?

Like Beardsley, Paul Henle also sees a twofold semantic relationship at
the heart of metaphorical meaning. Employing C. S. Peirce's definitions of
symbol and icon, Henle develops a suggestive contemporary variation of
the analogy approach: the iconic signification theory. As Henle explains
Peirce's distinction:

> A sign is a *symbol* insofar as it signifies according to an arbitrary rule, insofar as it is a
> conventional sign. [Peirce held the conventional to be essentially arbitrary.] A sign
> is an *icon* to the extent that it signifies in virtue of similarity. (In Johnson, p. 87)

Two types of road signs readily illustrate this distinction. One functions
symbolically, warning drivers in writing of children at play; the other sort,
an iconic sign in Peirce's sense, actually depicts the image of a child
tripping in the street.

According to Henle, metaphor

> is analyzable into a double sort of semantic relationship. First, using symbols in
> Peirce's sense, directions are given for finding an object or situation [this, according

to Henle, constitutes "ordinary" usage]. . . . Second, it is implied that any object or situation fitting the direction may serve as an icon of what one wishes to describe. The icon is never actually present [as in the road sign]; rather, through the rule, one understands what it must be [it is "described" in the sense that a "formula" is provided for "construction" of the icon] and, through this understanding, what it signifies. (In Johnson, p. 88)

The iconic signification theory posits the actuating moment of metaphor in the recognition of the iconic character of a word or phrase as it appears in the frame of "ordinary" usage. As in the controversion approach, the operation of metaphor is conceived, in the first instance, as a function of words in their denotative sense. It differs from the controversion theory in its assertion that metaphorical meaning is a result not of the perception of logical absurdity but of an "understanding" that a particular expression is figurative rather than strictly denotative in a given instance. That an icon signifies in virtue of similarity suggests an affinity between Henle's theory and classic comparison views. Searle, in fact, classifies Henle's approach as a comparison theory (see Ortony, p. 99). The mechanism, however, that Henle considers the means by which metaphorical meaning occurs, involving as it does "directions" in the semantic context for "construction" of the icon, is more complex than the apprehension of simple resemblance, which he notes can be asserted even between the number seventeen and an elephant ("in that they share the characteristics of being different from the moon"). Moreover, the iconic signification theory does not postulate any transfer of meaning between a metaphor and its semantic occasion, a function that many approaches which are at bottom comparison theories, such as Hrushovski's and Gumpel's, attribute to metaphor.

Henle's theory is tellingly critiqued by Israel Scheffler, who categorizes it as a "formulaic approach," one, that is, which presupposes

some formula (or manageable set of formulas) which, given available information about literal constituents, specifies in literal terms the meanings of metaphorical expressions (though not always within the bounds of their respective initial languages [as in Henle's theory, where specification is articulated iconically]). (*Beyond the Letter*, p. 92)

Scheffler discerns a basic problem with Henle's conception of the context-dependence of rules, the perception of pertinent similarities in the construal of iconically expressive metaphorical meaning. He indicates that the "context-by-context selection of the very criteria by which decoding is to proceed" reveals that despite his invocation of formula and directions, Henle fails to come up with any determinate rule explaining metaphorical meaning since, on the iconic signification account, "the mechanism [of any such explanation] operates through judgments of importance specific to varying contexts" (*Beyond the Letter*, p. 96). In other words, Henle cannot explain what it means to say that the iconic signification of metaphor is the result of apprehending directions or a formula, because *there are no criteria for a determinate formula, no basis for a generic set of directions* that can be extrapolated from the semantic occasions of different metaphors. Thus, there is no relevant ground for claiming that there is any formula in the first place.

   An influential theory that differs from those of Henle and Beardsley explains that metaphor is employed to communicate experience in a way that supersedes the hermeneutic mode of construal of "literal" language. This approach to metaphor, dubbed the supervenience theory by Beardsley, and called *intuitionism* by Scheffler, finds its most notable exponent in Philip Wheelwright. The heart of Wheelwright's conception of metaphor is what he distinguishes as "the double imaginative act of outreaching and combining . . . that essentially marks the metaphoric process." The two components of this "double imaginative act" are "epiphor," which Wheelwright explains as the "outreach and extension of meaning through comparison," and "diaphor," "the creation of new meaning by juxtaposition and synthesis."[39] Wheelwright's view is distinctive in postulating that the intuitive perception of new (synthesized) meaning results from the semantic " 'movement' . . . 'through' . . . certain particulars of experience (actual or imagined) in a fresh way . . . by juxtaposition [of words or phrases] alone" (p. 78).[40] The "diaphoric" stage is, in Warren Shibles's words, "directly opposed" (*An Analysis of Metaphor*, p. 66) to substitution views: no perception of resemblance of qualities or transfer of meaning is asserted. Wheelwright considers as an "ontological fact" the emergence, the simple coming into being, of "new qualities and new meanings . . . out of some hitherto ungrouped combination of elements" (p. 85). From the supervenience perspective, a metaphor is not replaceable by an "equivalent" literal meaning: the intuition is all. Essential as it is to the efficacy of the juxtaposition, the role of context is not the main focus of this approach. Supervenience theorists locate the ground of metaphorical meaning in cognitive experience governed by words in their connotative senses.[41] On this view, the phrase "Petals on a wet, black bough," from Pound's familiar "In a Station of the Metro," generates unique, intuitively apprehended, metaphorical meaning simply as a result of its juxtaposition to "The apparition of these faces in the crowd."

In addition to trenchant critiques of the comparison, interaction, and iconic signification theories, Israel Scheffler meticulously analyzes the supervenience, or "intuitionistic," approach. "Intuitionism," concedes Scheffler,

> is correct in holding that metaphors may bring additional powers of expression to the language in which they arise. Appeal to intuition, however, does nothing to explain how the understanding of metaphors is guided by past literal usage. (*Beyond the Letter*, p. 86)

Scheffler then raises some questions that clearly reveal what is deficient in any explanation of how metaphor operates that relies principally on the notion of intuition:

> How is the purportedly intuitive act [that Wheelwright maintains results from "diaphor": a semantic movement that he postulates as occurring through the "juxtaposition alone"] itself guided by prior divergent applications in understanding fresh metaphorical expressions? How can such guidance [presumably present in the metaphoric apprehension Wheelwright calls "epiphor": an "outreach and extension of meaning through comparison"], unmediated by formula, yet inform the grasp of the novel? Intuition is here no simple leap in the dark. . . . It is indeed creative and addressed to the hitherto unencountered, but it also builds upon prior understandings and past applications. (P. 87)

Considered in terms of Pound's couplet, Scheffler's criticism of intuitionistic theories would fault them for claiming that, as metaphor, "Petals on a wet, black bough" is apprehended intuitively, and for making that claim without accounting in any precise way for the indispensable role of "prior understandings and past applications" (of both clauses of the couplet and perhaps the title) in the metaphorical meaning of the phrase. Scheffler's point is that the appeal to intuition as a principle of explanation ignores what we might call the diachronic context of the realization of metaphor.

4. Contemporary Perspectives on Context:
Notes Toward a Contextual Theory of Metaphor

While Scheffler's consideration of metaphor in *Beyond the Letter* is largely
a series of critiques of various approaches, he does introduce his own
classification of the major theories.[42] Although the basis on which Scheffler discriminates between types of theories may be overfine in certain
instances, such as in his distinctions between the emotive and the intuitionistic views,[43] his perception that contextualism is a fundamental
category of metaphor theory (despite the fact that no theorist of metaphor
has specifically labeled his approach "contextualism") is significant for
two reasons. First, it calls attention to context, a key factor of metaphorical meaning (of all meaning for that matter), and the bearing of which
on metaphorical meaning every major theorist of metaphor considers in
some detail. Second, it suggests a realistic conceptual orientation for
practical approaches to metaphor, such as the one detailed in chapter 3,
which focuses on the pragmatics of metaphor in literary experience.

Although most theories call attention to the contextually determined
aspects of metaphorical meaning,[44] they do not go so far as to consider
context itself as the actual mechanism of metaphor. A thoroughgoing
contextualism would locate the ground of metaphorical meaning in the
semantic occasion of a figurative expression. While admitting of an interaction of some sort between a figure and its semantic setting, contextualism could not be expected, given the variability of context from instance
to instance, to venture a universal explanation (no "logic of explication
based on uniform principles of interpretation" [*Beyond the Letters*, p. 118])
that would provide a clue as to the nature of the interaction. This diverges
from the interactionism of Richards and Black, of course, who postulate
tenor/vehicle and frame/focus as generic interpretive schemas reflective
of the hypothesized interaction. Scheffler observes that although like the
interaction approach

> contextualism is prepared to recognize that metaphorical ascription varies in its force
> with variation in context . . . it offers no theory of commonplaces [the allusion is to
> specifics of Black's initial formulation of interactionism in *Models and Metaphors*]
> even as a presumptive account of the usual case. (P. 118)

For contextualism, there is no "usual case."
The two theories do share, however, an important similarity, one that is

fundamentally non-Aristotelian. Neither approach postulates that any form of equivalence, resemblance, or transfer is inherent in metaphor. Although he discerns crucial differences between interactionism and contextualism, Scheffler finds that Black's theory actually "verges on contextualism" to the extent that

> Some judgment of the context *is* implicitly presupposed as available to decide and, further, to determine the particular deviant implications [of a secondary subject (see Black, in Ortony, p. 28, for a summary of his position on the role of secondary subject in metaphor)]. (P. 118)

Contextualism also reveals a similarity to the controversion view in its claim that an expression is "metaphorical only if to some extent contra indicated" by context (*Beyond the Letter*, p. 119). It differs from the controversion account in that "some extent" of contraindication is not as extreme as the logical opposition of which Beardsley speaks. Two other less extreme characterizations of this aspect of metaphor are Ricoeur's "semantic impertinence" and Earl R. MacCormac's "semantic anomaly."[45]

A survey of observations by prominent theorists on the role of context in defining and understanding metaphor not only reveals a wide range of opinion about how metaphor functions but also provides a collection of suggestively related insights from which we can distil the elements of a coherent contextualist approach to metaphor. What follows is a series of statements on context in metaphor and, based on those statements, a provisional formulation of a contextual theory. The present section concludes with an assessment of this approach in light of an explication of a metaphor in George Herbert's lyric "Easter Wings."

Conceiving the context of metaphorical meaning as cognitive process, I. A. Richards describes metaphor as essentially

> an interaction between co-present thoughts, as I will call them, or, in terms of the context theorem, between different missing parts or aspects of the different contexts of a word's meaning. . . . a transaction between contexts. (*Philosophy of Rhetoric*, pp. 92–93)

Although this is a statement of Richards's interactionist stance, it makes plain his appreciation of the primacy of context in the process of metaphorical meaning.

Max Black indicates his sense of the centrality of context in the construal of metaphorical meaning when he affirms that

There are indefinitely many contexts (including nearly all the interesting ones) where the meaning of a metaphorical expression has to be reconstructed from the speaker's intentions (and other clues) because the broad rules of standard usage are too general to supply the information needed. (*Models and Metaphors*, p. 29)

Alluding to Donald Davidson's assertion that when "we try to say what a metaphor 'means,' we soon realize there is no end to what we want to mention" (in Sacks, p. 44), Merrie Bergmann articulates what she sees as "the grain of truth in Davidson's claim":

without knowing the context in which a metaphor occurs and who its author is, it is impossible to state conclusively what the metaphor "means" without drawing out all that it *could* mean. ("Metaphorical Assertions," p. 231)

A glance at the massive bibliographies of secondary literature that have grown around major works of literary art, even around specific metaphors (such as the "two-handed engine" of Milton's "Lycidas" alluded to in section 1), makes one skeptical of *ever* being able to state "conclusively" what an indefinite number of metaphors mean, despite considerable knowledge of both author and context.

In "The Metaphorical Twist," Monroe Beardsley accounts for the importance of context in the operation of metaphor when, in expounding his verbal-opposition theory, he describes the two elements of a "metaphorical attribution" as "a semantic distinction between two levels of meaning, and a logical opposition on one level" (in Johnson, p. 112). As operative in a metaphorical expression, this "semantic distinction" (that, recall, involves a logical opposition on the level where the metaphor is putatively perceived as an expression that, in view of standard usage, is illogical in the semantic context in which it appears) effects a shift, or "twist," from what that expression designates—its literal acceptation—to what it connotes—its figurative sense. According to Beardsley, the "potential range of connotations" depends as much upon the expression's literary context as it does upon anything the metaphor may mean exclusive of that context. Beardsley maintains that the complex of connotations that applies through metaphor to a particular literary context *transforms* that context and thereby establishes "a new contextual meaning" (*Aesthetics*, p. 143).[46]

For Paul Ricoeur the context of a metaphorical expression is a "familiar field of reference," grounding the directed working out of a meaning or "semantic aim." On the basis of this assumption Ricoeur explains the operation of metaphor in contextual terms by positing that

This already constituted meaning is raised from its anchorage in an initial field of reference and cast into the new referential field which it will then work to delineate.[47]

Probing metaphor from a different angle, Ted Cohen in "Metaphor and the Cultivation of Intimacy" asks whether the "magic of metaphors," rather than being a "matter of meaning of their words," might not actually be "a feature of the contexts of their use, of their 'pragmatics.' "[48] This approach to metaphor is untenable, however, as Cohen points out, without "the background of a general theory of meaning" (in Sacks, p. 4).[49]

In "On the Truth and Probity of Metaphor," Timothy Binkley's observations on the function of context in metaphorical meaning, going beyond Cohen's thoughts on the constitutive role of word use in how metaphor operates, focus on the problem of accounting for the pragmatics of the *analysis* of metaphor. Binkley contends that

> When someone wants to put forth an example of a use of language he exhibits an expression out of context. Sometimes he will specify at least part of the context in which we are to imagine the expression occurring, but even in these cases the expression is still out of its context of use. (In Johnson, p. 148)

In discussions of literary metaphor at least, this problem is on occasion obviated in instances where the entire work in which the metaphor occurs is presented and considered as a whole. For the context of use in analysis may subsume, and indeed enrich, that of a given instance of prereflective appreciation. Binkley's point is well taken, however, vis-à-vis theorists who develop their views on *how* metaphor means in light of trivial or what we might term "disembodied" metaphors.

Wayne Booth in "Metaphor as Rhetoric" envisages the structure of metaphors that "we care for most" as extending virtually indefinitely into the range of all the extratextual factors conceivable as components of their context. These metaphors, states Booth, "are always embedded in metaphoric structures that finally depend on and constitute selves and societies" (in Sacks, p. 61).

In a similar vein, Benjamin Hrushovski cautions that

> Semantic theory must overcome the "First-Sentence Fallacy"—the analysis of a sentence as if it stood alone. There are no first sentences in language. The "first sentences" of children are highly embedded in their (non-verbal) context. ("An Outline of Integrational Semantics," p. 61)

Finally, Mark Johnson, pondering the significance of context in the very recognition of metaphor, concludes that with a better understanding of "how features of context influence our interpretation of metaphor, we can get clearer about how we identify the metaphor in the first place" (*Philosophical Perspectives on Metaphor*, p. 24).

The foregoing observations on the significance of context in metaphorical meaning suggest the possibility of contextual approaches to metaphor predicated on one or more of the following postulations. Contextualism, as Scheffler notes, rejects any necessary "reliance on resemblance" (*Beyond the Letter*, p. 118). More fundamentally, a metaphorical expression is construable as metaphor in the first place only in some context in which that expression is embedded. As the extension (or range of reference) of metaphoric words constitutes a context of signification in itself, the mechanism of metaphor may be what Richards calls a "transaction" between contexts. Further, how a particular metaphor operates, or means, is a function not strictly of word meaning but of a potentially indefinite thematic context, one that focuses and thereby facilitates meaning. Metaphors that are not trivial, which includes all those that are interesting in literary experience,[50] are not isolated words, phrases, or sentences; they are always integral components of a universe of discourse. More than merely an articulation of discourse, however, metaphors can significantly modify the context that occasions them. On the other hand, it is the context that determines which predicates of the nonmetaphorical signification of a figurative expression have a bearing on that context.[51]

To assess the pragmatic implications of these contextualist assertions, consider the metaphorical expression, "the flight in me," in George Herbert's "Easter Wings":

Easter Wings

Lord, who createdst man in wealth and store,
Though foolishly he lost the same,
Decaying more and more,
Till he became
Most poor:
With thee
O let me rise
As larks, harmoniously,
And sing this day they victories:
Then shall the fall further the flight in me.

My tender age in sorrow did begin:
And still with sickness and shame
Thou didst so punish sin,
That I became
Most thin.
With thee
Let me combine,
And feel this day thy victory:
For, if I imp my wing on thine,
Affliction shall advance the flight in me.
(*The English Poems*, p. 63)

A radical contextualist, one holding that metaphor is nothing else than a component of meaning on the level of discourse (rather than a word- or sentence-level phenomenon), would consider "the flight in me" a senseless, unmetaphorical collection of words if Herbert's metaphor were abstracted from particular themes and images ("implicative complexes" in Black's terminology) associated with flight in the poem—such as salvation, Jesus' rising from the tomb, and man's redemption from his fallen state through the Savior's mediation. Another significant contextual factor that reveals the metaphor to be part of a larger frame of meaning is Herbert's placement of the expression: at the culmination of each of the two wing-shaped stanzas. Far from a trivial figure in the poem, "the flight in me" expresses near-ecstatic faith and hope by reason of the richly articulated and allusive complex of themes that constitute the aesthetic and religious occasion of the metaphor.

To claim that "the flight in me" functions metaphorically, not because of word meaning alone but as a result of its context, is credible enough, insofar as one accepts the view that the poetic frame of meaning has a unique semantic bearing on the phrase, regardless of what the words themselves might mean—or might be taken to mean (cf. Searle's notion of "utterance meaning," in Ortony, p. 93). Because word sense or the signification of any expression can differ in alternative contexts, it is the context that, as the situating factor of communication, fixes meaning and thus determines whether and in what sense a term is operating metaphorically. Guided by the principle that context determines which predicates of what is taken as an expression's literal meaning qualify the theme or themes that occasion it (what Black calls the "primary subject"), a contextualist could perceive "the flight in me" as dramatically connoting, for example, a heightened religious consciousness, an inspired escape from sin and decay, an elevated spiritual status achieved through grace.

From this perspective, then, "the flight in me" is comprehensible as nontrivial metaphor—"decodable" as such—only in context. Whether on this view the phrase removed from its context would even be identifiable as metaphor in the first place depends on how one understands the notion of *context*,[52] on how the phrase is understood, and on how one distinguishes metaphorical from literal meaning in the complex semantic frame that situates the expression and gives it point. Stripped of any salient semantic setting, the words "the flight in me" still signify particular things, although their collective meaning, being radically indeterminate, becomes trivially ambiguous.

Assuming that although metaphor is not a *component* of a larger frame of meaning it is nevertheless *possible* only through juxtaposed contexts of meaning (one being a unit of discourse and the other an expression in that unit of discourse), "the flight in me" is construable as a transaction *between* contexts or frames of reference (Hrushovski) or implicative complexes (Black).

At least two consequences of this position are unacceptable, however, to contextualism. First, contexts stand on this account as various configurations of meaning that metaphor somehow connects or relates (or of whose interconnection metaphor functions as an experiential index). The two contexts are the perceived literal and figurative[53] significations of the metaphor (a presupposition of comparison theories).[54] Alternatively, they may constitute (1) the semantic occasion of the phrase in the poem (obviously not identical with the expression's figurative meaning, and not inclusive of it) *and* (2) the meaning of the phrase in abstraction from that context (that, unlike merely the set of the phrase's literal meanings, includes other possible *figurative* significations). In either case, metaphor is logically distinct, if not autonomous, from context; and this suggests that metaphor is intelligible *exclusive of context*, a view, it should be clear, that is dubious at best, especially in light of practical hermeneutic exercises such as the explication of "the flight in me" in "Easter Wings."

Second, the effort to discern precisely *what* is being transacted between contexts combined with the enigma of *how* the transaction actually occurs assumes a clear distinction between the mechanism of metaphor (the transacting) and germane contexts. By identifying metaphor as a transaction between contexts, it is even arguable whether the view under discussion is in fact a version of contextualism: the contexts might actually be moments of some more comprehensive structural or organizational configuration of meaning, while the "transaction" termed "metaphor" could be merely the *whole* perceived from the *sum* (the aggregate or the "all") of its parts. As such, metaphor is a matter of perspective and less a principle of context than one of the con-formation of meanings in the thematic development of complete units of discourse. In terms of Herbert's metaphor this implies that "the flight in me," considered as a transaction between contexts, is a discrete figurative expression, a structural component that is not necessarily organic to the poem as a whole, even when it occurs in the closing line. On the other hand, when the poem is conceived as an evolving unity of meaning, "the flight in me" expresses the way two frames of reference—flight and spiritual elevation—fit together, con-form, in an Easter prayer of repentance and inspired hope, a religious meditation on the Fall and on redemption.

Abandoning Richards's notion of metaphor as a transaction between contexts does not, however, eliminate the possibility of a plausible contextual approach: metaphor can be understood as a function of the context that gives rise to it. And the explanation of exactly how a given metaphor expresses or amplifies the context that occasions it becomes, then, the meaning of contextualism. A contextualist interpretation of "the flight in me" might posit, for instance, that the expression operates metaphorically by rendering exuberant and intensely personal its thematic context of individual salvation through Christ. The plausibility of this interpretation lies in recognizing "flight" not as an incentive for suggestive comparisons but as actually denoting an escape from fallenness, a condition of spiritual ascendance—as an ecstatic sense of heightening spiritual awareness.

Discounting versions that incorporate such untenable assumptions as transfer or transaction, the practicability of contextualism makes it preferable to comparison and interaction views, at least as an account of literary metaphor. It does not murder literary experience by dissecting it, whether linguistically, semiotically, or in some other fashion; rather, it focuses on the dynamic, interdependent lines of evolving meaning—the thematic context—that occasion literary metaphor and provide the only valid framework for evaluating what it does in a work of literary art. (Determining how literary metaphor does what it does requires taking into account a different frame of reference, as I shall explain.)

The most glaring weakness of an otherwise workable contextualism, a problem that neither interactionism nor comparison theories definitively address, is the inability to explain how a metaphor like "the flight in me" articulates the themes that occasion it. This suggests the cardinal point that the credibility and hence the value of explanations of what metaphor does (its "effects") depend upon—presuppose insight into—how metaphor does it.[55] We return then to what Black, in "How Metaphors Work," concludes is the basic and still-unresolved problem of metaphor: the issue of what it means "to say that in a metaphor one thing is thought of (or viewed) *as* another thing" (in Sacks, p. 192).

5. *Conclusion*

The preceding discussion should make evident the need for a more satisfactory approach to literary metaphor. The inherent difficulty of the views touched on in the foregoing sections is that they typically grow out of insights into the efficacy of metaphor, that is, what metaphor does. With respect to how, theorists tend to base the application of their favored analytic schemas on impressions or unexamined concepts (transfer, for instance, or transaction) that they take as adequate representations of the way metaphor operates. This is a theoretical misstep that, to repeat George E. Yoos's trenchant perception, involves turning uncritically "from the question of what a metaphor is like descriptively to the question of what we are doing in the name of interpretation." Attempts to account for the mechanism of metaphorical meaning in terms of the conditions that give rise to it are too infrequent.[56] One result of this trend in metaphor theory is that the conceptual schemes of standard views are built upon unexplained foundational, or "root,"[57] metaphors such as "comparison," "substitution," "transfer," "analogy," and "interaction." These seminal interpretive metaphors remain unexplained because they are inexplicable in the same realm of discourse in which the theory based on them is articulated. How, for instance, is metaphorical transfer between frames of reference[58] to be explained semantically, without recourse to circular reasoning, if a semantic interpretation of metaphor presupposes transfer as the very principle that makes interpretation itself intelligible?

This uncritical use of metaphor to account for how metaphor *means* calls to mind the physicist W. H. Watson's discerning analysis of the confusion of thought generated by the spatial representation of time.[59] Watson explains that

the succession of points along a line only in one direction corresponds to the succession of instants of time. . . . In the motion [of a particle along a straight line],

this line is traversed in the direction away from the origin in time. We are tempted to
say that the same line considered in opposite sense [*sic*] (i.e., toward the origin)
represents the "motion of the particle backward in time" instead of saying that the
line viewed in this way does not represent a process at all. The logic of "before:after"
does not allow sense to the form of the words "backward in time" any more than the
geometry of the sphere allows its orthogonal projection on a plane to cover the whole
plane. Nevertheless, literary grammar (as opposed to logic) appears to sanction the
expression "backward in time". . . . The very fact that in speaking of temporal
relations we use words whose application properly belongs to space ought to warn us
that, when we have these terms in mind, we use a spatial representation of time. (In
Danto and Morgenbesser, pp. 227–28)

This extended passage from a piece in a collection of essays on the
philosophy of science is pertinent on two counts to the study of how
metaphors *mean*. First, it suggests the fallacy of supposing that rhetorical
or linguistic or semiotic explanations of literary metaphor are sufficient or
even appropriate insofar as what given metaphors mean inheres in a realm
of experience that transcends the categories of rhetoric or linguistics or
semiotics. Hans-Georg Gadamer goes so far as to assert that

The structure, grammar, syntax of a language—all those factors which linguistic
science makes thematic—are not at all conscious to living speaking. . . . A really
gigantic achievement of abstraction is required of everyone who will bring the
grammar of his native language to explicit consciousness. The actual operation of
language lets grammar vanish entirely behind what is said in it at any given time.
. . . The more language is a living operation, the less we are aware of it. Thus it
follows from the self-forgetfulness of language that its real being consists in what is
said in it. What is said in it constitutes the common world in which we live and to
which belongs also the whole great chain of tradition reaching us from the literature
of foreign languages, living as well as dead. The real being of language is that into
which we are taken up when we hear it—what is said. (*Philosophical Hermeneutics*,
pp. 64–65)

Second, if Watson's statement is considered in light of the prominent
theories cited in this chapter, it reveals the inaccuracy of approaches to
metaphor that assume or overtly postulate notions—what Walter J. Ong
would term "analytic thought structures"—such as "transfer" or an "interaction" involving "vehicles" and "frames," "filtering" and "movement."
Although this imagery is heuristically suggestive, it does not provide a
cogent experiential description of how metaphors operate. Meaning is not

manifest in, nor does it necessarily develop in conformance with, the spatial or temporal modalities that the imagery cited expresses: an extended sentence or thought can mean less than a single word or a flash of insight. Ong makes the same point in a different way when, in his study "Literate Orality of Popular Culture," he explains that "the medium is not the message, for one medium will incarnate many messages" (*Rhetoric, Romance, and Technology*, p. 290).

To avoid arbitrary and misleading interpretive inferences in working out the basis of a practicable approach to literary metaphor, analysis must take as its starting point not *metaphorical meaning* as such[60] but *the meaning of metaphorical meaning*.[61] In this connection Alfred Tarski's well-known correspondence theory of truth[62] has instructive bearing on both the critical and the constructive aspects of the present study. Tarski's insight that an expression's truth is knowable only if the semantics of its language (the system of meaning that fixes the relation between a descriptive expression and its reference) constitutes a metalanguage, a fundamentally more inclusive domain, has significant implications for understanding (1) how metaphor means and (2) for the theoretical limits of conceptually grounded, or analytical (as opposed to phenomenologically experiential) approaches to metaphor.

1. In order to have any coherent relation to fact, an "object language" (denotative, literal language) must be integrated in a metalanguage, a semantic system that designates what the words of the object language mean when they are true of anything—what sense they make.[63] To the degree that in its pragmatics—its communicative context—a metaphorical expression transcends denotative sense, it is a metalinguistic phenomenon conveying the meaning of what it denotes in that context. In this connection it would be reasonable to conclude that the metalanguage, or semantic ground of *literary* metaphor, is literary experience—a realm of meaning that contains the truth of literary metaphor.

2. The implications of Tarski's theory of truth for a meaningful theory of metaphor are crucial. If the language of a given view of metaphor is not grounded in a more comprehensive, or "higher order," domain of meaning—one that serves as the reservoir of objective sense of any statement made in that language—no intelligible way of ascertaining the certainty of any of its claims about metaphor is possible: the approach will be viciously circular in its reliance on unanalyzed primitive concepts—substitution, for example, or transfer or interaction. As Karl Popper states in his summary of Tarski's theory, "Every sufficiently rich language speaking

about some subject matter may . . . contain its own 'morphology' and 'syntax,' while (as Tarski has shown) no consistent language may contain the means of defining its own semantics" (*Objective Knowledge*, p. 327).

It follows from this that coherent theories of metaphor must make sense in a richer order of meaning than that of their discursive formulations of the nature of the metaphoric process. Appealing to specific instances of metaphor to illustrate meaning in a gesturelike manner only results in vacuous circularity: the meaning of metaphor is what the metaphor means. On the other hand, to regard systems of rhetoric,[64] say, of semiotics, or of grammar,[65] as the metalanguage of discourse about metaphor is to restrict the scope of the possible meaning of what can be claimed about how metaphor functions (whether in aesthetics or in scientific speculation) to a distortingly narrow context. Clearly *some* realm of discourse must merit acceptance if coherent observations about how metaphors mean are to be made. Yet, since no fully intelligible theory of metaphor can account in its own terms (without being circular) for its postulations about metaphorical meaning and at the same time ignore prereflective understanding as to the meaning of those postulates, the first requirement of a cogent theory is to provide an account of the prereflective apprehension invoked in its assertions about metaphor. As Stanley Rosen makes clear in *Limits of Analysis*, "it is impossible to intentionally utter a meaningful proposition [such as one that explains how metaphor means] without an understanding of what it means to say something of something" (p. 52).

The question then is where should the study of the meaning of metaphorical meaning begin? No indisputable claim is possible for some ultimate ground of meaning, some absolutely definitive interpretation of meaning of any sort. It seems to me we must begin with the concept of *importance*. Considerations of what is of importance, linked as they are to specific purposes, provide a guide for analysis.[66] The principal end in the case of literary art is the precise communication of vital experience in all of its dramatic, presentational immediacy. The participation in vital experience as it is communicated narratively[67]—in the medium of what Herbert Read calls "poetic thinking"[68]—serves in what follows as a definition of literary experience, a definition that when elaborated provides an intelligible phenomenological frame of reference for construing the meaning of literary metaphor. In accounting for the meaning of metaphorical meaning, this approach will shed light on the cause, the occasioning, of literary metaphor and will afford a conceptual basis for a practicable, experiential perspective on how metaphors mean.

CHAPTER TWO

Literary Experience

A PHENOMENOLOGICAL VIEW

The particular intention that directs the system
of language functioning in metaphorical utterances includes a
demand for elucidation to which we can respond only by approaching
the semantic possibilities of this discourse with a different
range of articulation, the range of speculative discourse.

PAUL RICOEUR
The Rule of Metaphor

1. The Phenomenological Character of Literary Experience

The participation in vital experience as it gets communicated through literary art is a view of literary experience readily amenable to a phenomenological analysis.[1] "Phenomenological" need not refer to any systematic philosophy, such as that of Husserl or Heidegger. As employed in the present study it simply indicates an orientation that stresses the primacy of presentational awareness, the primacy of prediscursive apprehension of the "life-world" (*Lebenswelt*).[2] Perhaps the most striking feature of phenomenological awareness is its quality of immediacy, in which objects of the imagination possess all the irrefragable presence of sense impressions. The pertinence of a phenomenological approach to literary experience becomes clear when we reflect that literary art communicates as literature through expressive, as opposed to discursive, utterances and that, as C. I. Lewis discerns, the reference of expressive statements "terminates in the immediate and phenomenological" (*Analysis of Knowledge and Valuation*, p. 397).[3]

A phenomenological approach thus presupposes primitive, aesthetic

immediacy to be the fundamental epistemic modality of literary experience.[4] The deliberative construal of meaning employed in literary analysis
is discrete from and secondary to direct experience. Further, when extrinsic contexts of meaning are imposed on reading for purposes of explanation "the [aesthetic] effect is extinguished, because the effect is in the
nature of an experience and not an exercise in explanation."[5] Literary
experience is thus readily distinguishable from the analytic frame of mind
on epistemic grounds—the way of knowing is different in each case.

This is not to say that literary experience is devoid of knowledge
acquired through analysis nor even that analysis is not a tacit component of
literary experience.[6] Few readers familiar with the literature would deny
that analysis of, say, biographical details of Charlotte Brontë's life during
the period she composed *Shirley* or of the literary historical milieu in which
Whitman's *Leaves of Grass* first appeared may significantly enhance literary experience. The acquisition of knowledge that enriches the context of
signification of a literary work (the complex of meanings and associations it
vivifies) is typically, though by no means exclusively, a matter of analytic
deliberation and dialogue and of intertextual study. On the other hand, it is
doubtless as often the case that previous literary experience that has not
been amplified or mediated by overt critical activity also contributes to the
context of signification of a literary work.

As the apprehension of all sorts of emotional and conceptual meaning,
literary experience is a form of aesthetic perception that is instinct with
elements generally associated with analytic thought. In *Visual Thinking*,
Rudolph Arnheim identifies analytic operations as actual components of
perception:

> the cognitive operations called thinking are not the privilege of mental processes
> above and beyond perception but the essential ingredient of perception itself.
> I am referring to such operations as active explanation, selection, grasping of
> essentials, simplification, abstraction, analysis and synthesis, completion, correc-
> tion, comparison, problem solving as well as combining, separating, putting in
> context. (P. 13)[7]

The relevance of Arnheim's observation for literary experience is perhaps best appreciated in light of the distinction between "understanding"
and "interpretation." While perception as a form of understanding may
involve a variety of built-in interpretive operations,[8] interpretation is not a
precondition of aesthetic perception nor, therefore, of literary experience.
Laurent Stern substantiates this position when he points out that "Since we

understand at least some interpretations without further interpretation, understanding an interpretation cannot require a never ending chain of further interpretations."[9] To state that literary experience attests to discursive thought is thus not to identify it with—nor to presume that it is reducible to—processes of analytic thinking (interpretation). Identifying the literary experience of reading a poem or a novel with the tacit analytic components that make possible the reading, which is itself an overtly analytic endeavor, is like equating the life of a person with the physiological processes that make it possible and sustain it. Analyses of literary meaning, carried out in terms of what atomistic grammatical, linguistic, or semiotic units signify, generally yield reductive interpretations. This is so because the rules of construal are internal to grammatical or linguistic or semiotic frames of meaning and not necessarily to those frames of meaning inherent in any given piece of literary art.[10] To paraphrase A. N. Whitehead: analysis destroys its usefulness when it indulges in brilliant feats of explaining away.

Phenomenological facts stand as things-in-themselves only in presentational immediacy, where they are unmediated by efforts at explanations or by the epistemological assumptions underlying the methodology or rationale of formal explanation. As soon as we begin to reflect upon experience—applying analytic concepts, theories, or strategies in order to construe meaning—and attempt to *make* sense rather than merely to *take* the phenomenological sense of it, we are no longer directly engaged, con-forming—no longer *in formation*, as it were—with the original facts as phenomena of experience.[11] As Stanley Rosen observes, "the cognitive content of a perception is acquired directly, as if through mere 'presence' of the sensed object, and not by the mediation of discursive analysis" (*Limits of Analysis*, p. 16).[12] Maurice Merleau-Ponty astutely traces the way that analytic thought in effect operates at a conscious remove from experience that is phenomenologically immediate:

> Analytic reflection starts from our experience of the world and goes back to the subject as to a condition of possibility distinct from that experience, revealing the all-embracing synthesis as that without which there would be no world. To this extent it ceases to remain part of our experience and offers, in place of an account, a reconstruction. (*Essential Writings*, p. 30)

From a phenomenological perspective, then, the aesthetics of perception underlies, indeed presupposes, any act of interpretation.[13]

The preceding observations afford a compelling philosophical rationale for the contention that aesthetic perception in its primitive, living immediacy is the primary (if not the only) epistemic modality of literary experience. Actual living, not past or "virtual" life, is communicated phenomenologically through the experience of literary art. An inquiry into this aspect of the phenomenology of literary experience needs to be experiential in focus and tenor if it is to avoid being reductive. For this reason terms like *importance, presentational immediacy, conformation,* and *enactment*—hopelessly vague for formal logical, semiotic, or linguistic exegeses—serve in the present study as touchstones for conveying a felt, a lived, understanding of flesh-and-blood awareness. As Fritz Kaufmann put it,

> [phenomenology] never loses the colors of life, the dynamics of consciousness which it is in search of—the concrete experience from which mere objectification and subjectification, mere construction and reconstruction are alienated. (In Schilpp, p. 810)

The concrete, sensuous immediacy of acts of physical and perceptual engagement typifies literary experience as well, and it is a principal means by which literary art communicates its conceptual content. [14] The depictive imagery that begins in the fourth stanza of Wallace Stevens's "The Motive for Metaphor" vividly illustrates this:

The Motive for Metaphor

You like it under the trees in autumn,
Because everything is half dead.
The wind moves like a cripple among the leaves
And repeats words without meaning.

In the same way, you were happy in spring,
With the half colors of quarter-things,
The slightly brighter sky, the melting clouds,
The single bird, the obscure moon—

The obscure moon lighting an obscure world
Of things that would never be quite expressed,
Where you yourself were never quite yourself
And did not want nor have to be,

Desiring the exhilarations of changes:
The motive for metaphor, shrinking from

> The weight of primary noon,
> The A B C of being,
>
> The ruddy temper, the hammer
> Of red and blue, the hard sound—
> Steel against intimation—the sharp flash,
> The vital, arrogant, fatal, dominant X.
>
> *(Collected Poems,* p. 288)

The explicitly conveyed conceptual content of the first, discursive, part of the poem is about a particular sort of enjoyment that is the motive for metaphor. In the opening stanza this enjoyment is identified with an apprehension of the "half-dead" things of autumn and of the intimations of the wind that "repeats words without meaning." In the next quatrain the concept of this metaphor-engendering happiness is further amplified in the context of springtime experiences. Like its counterpart autumn, spring is a transitional period, and to enjoy it is to respond to the suggestion of fulfillment, to things incompletely realized: "half colors of quarter-things, / The slightly brighter sky." The third stanza concerns the subjective correlates of the pleasurable objective perceptions. An "obscure moon"—Stevens's symbol of the imagination—lights an obscure world of half-meanings, "things that would never be quite expressed." These suggestions of meaning involve the self, whose identity in the world of imaginative half-light is transitional, never quite fixed. The desire for "the exhilarations of changes," in the self as well as in nature, is in a positive sense the motive for metaphor.

In characterizing the motivation for metaphor in negative terms, Stevens turns in the second part of the poem (the fourth and fifth stanzas) from discursive, conceptually explicit description to the prediscursive, intrinsically poetic communication of ideas in a series of metaphors bound to the image of "shrinking from." "Primary noon" and "The A B C of being," for example, dramatically present (rather than describe) the concepts of stark, fixed clarity and radical, reductive simplicity from which the form of desire that conduces to metaphor "shrinks." As the closing line of the poem suggests, the exhilarations that mark the fulfillment of such desire depend on the evasion of arrogantly definite meanings that dominate, and thereby prove fatal to, imaginative life.

This sensuously immediate communication of the conceptual is the literary artist's—the maker's—way of humanizing the world. In the words of Northrop Frye,[15]

Literature's world is a concrete human world of immediate experience. The poet uses images and objects and sensations much more than he uses abstract ideas [which, as I argue, he *depicts* by means of sensuously immediate images]; the novelist is concerned with telling stories, not with working out arguments. The world of literature is human in shape, a world where the sun rises in the east and sets in the west over the edge of a flat earth in three dimensions, where the primary realities are not atoms or electrons but bodies, and the primary forces are not energy or gravitation but love and death and passion and joy. (*Educated Imagination*, pp. 27–28)

The concrete phenomenological world of literary experience that Frye describes is inherently processive and organically integrated.[16] The dynamic of literary experience is a function of the reader's processes of perceptual awareness, a condition of the tempo and tensions of conscious apprehension. Jean-Paul Sartre likens the "literary object" to "a peculiar top which exists only in movement. To make it come into view a concrete act called reading is necessary, and it lasts only as long as this act can last." As Sartre puts it, "the literary object has no other substance than the reader's subjectivity" (*Literature and Existentialism*, p. 45).[17] The pace, however, at which the reader "follows" a narrative, and in so doing actualizes its temporality (rendering the sequence of events, for instance, an actual sequence and thus more than merely an abstract pattern), is inextricably tied to thematic and stylistic elements of a text. As Sartre observes, "Raskolnikov's waiting is *my* waiting which I lend him. Without this impatience of the reader he would remain only a collection of signs" (p. 45). Thus while a narrative contributes to the rate at which events unfold for a reader, *that* they unfold in the first place is a condition of the dynamic medium of their actualization: the reader's living awareness.[18]

The unity of literary experience attests to the holistic configuration of the deliverances of aesthetic perception.[19] In this connection Susanne Langer makes a perceptive point about organic structure in the arts:

what [a work of art] renders in its own logical projection must be true in design to the structure of experience. That is why art seems essentially organic. . . . It must be remembered, of course, that a work of art is not an actual organism, but presents only the appearance of life, growth, and functional unity. . . . But just because the created appearance is all that has organic structure, a work of art shows us the *appearance* of life; and the semblance of functional unity is indispensable if the illusory tension pattern is to connote felt tensions, human experience. (*Feeling and Form*, p. 373)

Langer astutely discerns here that the organic character of aesthetic experience is extrinsic (as a "logical projection") to the material basis of works of art. She overlooks, however, the communicative context in which art engenders that experience and so in effect factors out the living components of art (what in literary experience the reader's act of reading contributes).[20]

I have asserted that in literary experience the quality with which literary art communicates its conceptual content is concretely, sensuously immediate. This aesthetic immediacy calls for explication in order to clarify how the objectification of the conceptual content of literature is the epistemological basis of literary experience. (Pursuing this line of thought is essential in formulating a cogent account of the depictive character of metaphor, one that helps to elucidate how metaphor functions in literary experience.)

How then is the immediacy of literary experience—what Frye calls the "concrete human world of immediate experience"—articulated? To postulate that on the most fundamental level the immediacy of literary experience is a structure of space or time, or of both, is of little help. The contents of imaginative activity cannot be localized in any conventional spatiotemporal sense: the realms of fancy are not happenings of space; they are no-where. And the apprehension of proportion[21] at the heart of the spatiality of imagined space is the realization of inferences based on recollected experience in actual space. Despite the temporal connotations of the term *immediate* (and while presupposed as a condition of the possibility of communication as, indeed, is spatiality) determinations of time, on the other hand, are coordinates of change and as such antithetical to the fixity of immediacy, that is, to what facilitates coherence and focus.[22] Käte Hamburger astutely describes the assimilation in the novel of spatial and temporal apperception in the presentational aspect of literary experience:

> Fictive time, the present, the past, and future of the persons in the novel, comes to be experienced when it is formed as such, *when it is elaborated through those presentational means open to narration:* just as space only then appears in the novel when it is narrated into it. (*Logic of Literature*, p. 93; emphasis added)[23]

This view may seem at first to contradict the claim made earlier that literary experience is inherently processive; however, the difference between the temporal structure of the process of literary experience and, to anticipate, the thematic structure of the qualitative (dramatic) immediacy of that experience parallels that between the uniformly moving frames of a film and the thematically fixed images projected on the screen.

In an elegant phenomenological analysis of perception, Ernst Cassirer reveals the nonspatial, atemporal nature of conceptual unity of the sort that operates as a principle of coherence in literary experience. Taking a house as the object of awareness, Cassirer explains that

> [it] is not given in a single perception; it contains a whole class of perceptions that are combined with each other and related to each other by a definite rule [in literary experience, a theme]. According to the greater or smaller distance from the observer, according to his point of view, his special perspective, according to the various conditions of illumination the appearance of a house incessantly changes its shape. But all these widely different appearances are nevertheless thought to be the representation of one and the same "object," of an identical thing. (*Symbol, Myth, and Culture: Essays and Lectures of Ernst Cassirer 1935–1945*, p. 152)[24]

Rudolph Arnheim attributes this determinateness of the object to the element of continuity in change: "as object and observer move around in space the retinal projection goes through a gradual, perfectly organized modification of size, and the continuity of this process preserves the identity of the object in spite of the change of size" (*Visual Thinking*, p. 42).

To evaluate how the immediacy of the human world is articulated in literary experience in light of a literary example, consider the following passage from Swiss novelist and playwright Max Frisch's *Homo Faber:*

> I've often wondered what people mean when they talk about an experience. I'm a technologist and accustomed to seeing things as they are. I see everything they are talking about very clearly, after all, I'm not blind. I see the moon over the Tamaulipas desert—it is more distinct than at other times, perhaps, but still a calculable mass circling round our planet, an example of gravitation, interesting, but in what way an experience? I see the jagged rocks, standing out black against the moonlight; perhaps they do look like the jagged backs of prehistoric monsters, but I know they are rocks, stone, probably volcanic, one would have to examine them to be sure of this. Why should I feel afraid? There aren't any prehistoric monsters any more. Why should I imagine them? . . . I am shivering, but I know that in seven to eight hours the sun will be shining again. What is all this about the end of the world? I can't imagine a lot of nonsense, merely in order to experience something. (Pp. 21–23)

The depicted space of the desert in which engineer Walter Faber contemplates "experience" near his downed airliner is not the principle that organizes the way the scene is depicted. Rather, it is a function—an indeterminate one—of an arrangement of images. The moon is over the desert; the rocks stand out in the moonlight. How high the moon appears over the desert, the direction in which Faber is facing, and how far the rocks loom would provide additional locational cues, but they are not factored into the arrangement and so are not features of the space of the scene. Even if Frisch had described in minute detail the spatial configuration of the setting, the arrangement of imagery still would be in the first instance a matter of thematic, as opposed to spatial, exigency.

The temporality of the scene is the flow and sequence of thoughts and images perceived as composing the consciousness of a defensively cynical technological positivist. How long does Faber gaze at the moon? How long does he spend in contemplation? Regardless of how Frisch had indicated the periods of time, the answer for literary experience must be: Long enough. The sensuously immediate deliverances (including the sense of duration) of the depiction of the moonlit desert night is hardly more than incidentally an expression of temporal process. In the aesthetic immediacy of literary experience the suspension (in principle) of process does not disintegrate the unity of experience, since literary experience is *thematically* structured, whereas in the context of process or flux, temporality is the seminal constitutive category, and the suspension of action spells the dissolution of unity and coherence.

Given that the aesthetic immediacy of literary experience, although amenable to analysis in spatial and temporal terms, is articulated neither spatially nor temporally,[25] it is necessary to turn to a more abstract explanatory principle. When alternative concepts such as spatiality and temporality prove insufficient for explaining a given phenomenon (in this case, the perceptual immediacy of the human "life-world" that characterizes the epistemology of literary experience), it is prudent to evaluate the problem by considering the phenomenon in light of constitutive principles that the alternative concepts share. One such principle that underlies the intelligibility of both space and time and that affords insight into the aesthetic immediacy of literary experience is the notion of "extension."[26]

As Whitehead describes it, extension "is that general scheme of relationships providing the capacity that many objects can be welded into the real unity of one experience" (*Process and Reality*, p. 67). In the domain of literary experience this "general scheme" or pattern of relationships that facilitates unified presentation involves the play of ideas, characters, and actions that constitute the thematic form (or from a temporal perspective, the development) of a literary work. And the immediacy of literary experience (a condition of the reader's conscious entertainment of that form), wherein "many objects"—everything from phonemes to cultural myths— are integrated in a unified presentational field, is clearly extensive.

The section that follows probes in some detail the epistemology of this extensive immediacy by investigating how what is apparent in literary experience is manifest in awareness. The aim is to articulate a cogent phenomenological rationale for the account in chapter 3 of how metaphor operates as a depictive image in literary experience. While the analysis in section 2 is somewhat involved and philosophically technical, the chapter summary affords a succinct overview of the main points developed in the discussion as they contribute to a phenomenological view of literary experience.

2. The Presentational Immediacy of Literary Experience

This section makes explicit the philosophical foundations of the literary aesthetic conceived in this study as a frame of reference for construing literary metaphor phenomenologically as a depictive image. A. N. Whitehead is the philosopher to whose thought the present analysis is most indebted and whose work contains fundamental insights into the epistemology of what I take to be the presentational immediacy of literary experience. The exposition that follows of this complex form of presentational immediacy develops in light of an explication of Whitehead's conceptions of *presentational immediacy, causal efficacy,* and *symbolic reference.* Whitehead's views on valuation will also be considered. They are pertinent to the discussion in that they help to clarify the interdependence of apprehension and meaning in literary experience.

Analysis of what Whitehead understands as presentational immediacy and causal efficacy facilitates explication of the perceptual epistemology of presentational awareness. Without appeal to spatial or temporal categories, it reveals how the extensional aspect of presentational literary experience conveys the interconnectedness of the "objects" that it integrates "in the unity of one experience." The *presentational immediacy of literary experience,* however, is an order of awareness that is *less primitive* than either simple presentational immediacy or causal efficacy, the two "pure" modes of perception whose interrelation ("symbolic reference") Whitehead takes to be the basis of symbolic meaning: for literary experience is nothing if not a function of symbolic meaning.

In the most general sense, the aesthetically immediate is what is *present* for perception—not symbolically, but actually.[27] The aesthetically immediate may be the words on a page, or some other form (either discrete or mixed) of sensuous image or abstract idea. The phenomenological data of aesthetic perception are present as fundamental, qualitative components of awareness. In literary experience the dramatic articulation of literary themes is what renders them perceptible as phenomena, and thus as primitive and compelling in awareness as our apprehension of sensuous quality. Before turning to elements of the characteristically dramatic nature of the literary aesthetic, however, I want to explore in some depth the epistemology of aesthetic perception vis-à-vis Whitehead's concepts of presentational immediacy, causal efficacy, and symbolic reference.

Following this phase of the inquiry, chapter 3 takes up the function of literary metaphor in the presentational dimension of literary experience, 1) showing literary metaphor to operate wholly within nondiscursive, literary experience and in so doing 2) outlining an experiential context from which to determine the appropriate parameters of discursive, analytic thinking in the apprehension and construal of metaphorical meaning.

As already noted, the concept of the *presentational immediacy of literary experience* derives largely from Whitehead, principally from his classic discussions of presentational immediacy and causal efficacy in the University of Virginia's Barbour-Page Lectures for 1927, published as *Symbolism: Its Meaning and Effect,* and in the 1927–28 Gifford Lectures, which evolved into his magnum opus, *Process and Reality.*[28] In *Symbolism* Whitehead describes perception in the mode of presentational immediacy as

> a physical fact which may, or may not, enter into consciousness. Such entry will depend on attention and on the activity of conceptual functioning whereby physical experience and conceptual imagination are fused into knowledge. (P. 16)

Since the qualitative content of awareness, an irrefragable deliverance that originates as such in awareness, is characteristic of the presentationally immediate data of literary experience, the notion of presentational immediacy *as it pertains to the literary aesthetic* is restricted in its applica-

tion to the domain of conscious awareness. Literary experience is consequently what Whitehead would term "high-grade" functioning of a "high-
grade" organism.

Although he states that presentational immediacy is "our perception of
the contemporary world by means of the senses" (*Process and Reality*, p.
311), Whitehead has more in mind than simple sense impressions such as
the deliverances of sight or hearing. Presentational immediacy is a physical "feeling" that "acquires integration with the valuation inherent in its
conceptual realization as a type of experience" (p. 311). In other words,
"valuation" is an essential component of the very conception of anything
that is present for awareness.[29] And given the epistemological orientation
of the present inquiry, it is perhaps best understood as the experiential
index of our participation in the world, indeed, of our formative relations
(both those we take as constituting our selves and the relations that we
perceive as generating the data of experience as they are present for us) to
whatever we experience. This view is implicit in Whitehead's description
of presentational immediacy as, "our immediate perception of the contemporary external world, appearing as an element constitutive of our own
experience" (*Symbolism*, p. 21).[30] Thus although he identifies presentational immediacy with sense perception, Whitehead has in mind a phenomenon that is at once more comprehensive and more determinate.[31]

As a conception of sense perception modified to include valuation,
presentational immediacy suggests the epistemology of a literary experience that communicates the value-structured, "concrete human world," in
Northrop Frye's words, "of immediate experience" (*The Educated Imagination*, p. 27).[32]

Whitehead's understanding of valuation is comprehensive and reflects
the cosmological reach of his thought; he regards it as a complex phenomenon that attests to the interplay of all elements of the universe.[33] What is
relevant to an understanding of the order of presentational immediacy at
the core of literary experience is that valuation is a litmus of what Whitehead calls the "solidarity"[34]—the organic interrelatedness—of an object
of awareness (in literary experience an image, idea, or motif) with the
subject aware of it, and that the relation acquires its sense, its meaning, in
terms of the nature, or point of view, of the subject.[35] As a principle
then of perspective, valuation is directly related to—in fact underlies the
formulation of—that which appears to us self-evident in presentational
experience, including that which is presentationally immediate in literary
experience. The presentational immediacy of literary experience is thus

inherently evaluative and as such constitutes a participative mode of awareness, where evaluation—instinct in the very process of apprehending—attests to an active engagement with literary art. Literary experience is more than merely a passive witnessing of situations and ideas, personalities and motifs: it stands as a *bearing witness* to the content of literature, as a commitment of the most personal sort. The willing suspension of disbelief calls for no less.

Whitehead posits presentational immediacy as one of two correlative pure modes of perception that, along with "the mode of conceptual analysis," structure the concrete actuality of human experience. A look at causal efficacy, the second type of perception, is essential for distinguishing how the presentational immediacy of literary experience is what Whitehead would term a complex or "mixed" version of presentational immediacy.

Whitehead understands the perception of causal efficacy as the sense or feeling of how things interrelate. "Anger, hatred, fear, terror, attraction, love, hunger, eagerness, massive enjoyment" are experiences that attest to "the clearest recognition of other actual things reacting upon ourselves" (*Symbolism*, p. 45); they are indexes of causal connectedness.

Perception of any sort means a subjective awareness of facts. The facts may be words on a page, their extension, their etymology, their syntax, or their place in the rhyme-scheme of a Spenserian sonnet. The awareness might be a vagueness bordering on incomprehension or an intense, sophisticated appreciation born of the rhythmic, etymological, thematic, and literary significations and resonances of the words. Regardless of clarity, accuracy, and scope, however, a subjective awareness could be said to "conform" with literary form to the degree that such form becomes a factor in the apprehension of what appears self-evident, that is, what is presentationally immediate, in the reading of a literary text. Literary experience is an activity in which the aesthetic perception (regardless of the degree of its historic, thematic, or semantic perspicacity) of the engaged, the committed, reader is how the reader conforms with a text.[36] Conformation in this sense is what in a different context David Norton calls "participatory enactment,"[37] and what in the first volume of *Time and Narrative* Paul Ricoeur defines in more general terms as "our connection to the plot's [or theme's] capacity to model experience" (p. 76). Conforming with a literary text reveals the seminal role of literary form in the actualization of meaning in literary experience. *How* a reader conforms with a text—due largely and in general to its formal characteristics—is the way it acquires literary meaning and how, consequently, it becomes for the reader a literary experience.

Focusing on conformation as a metaphysical principle, Whitehead draws a conclusion that supports the contention that form plays an originative function in the meaning of literary experience. "There can be," he declares, "no useful aspect of anything unless we admit the principle of conformation, whereby what is already made becomes a determinant of what is in the making" (*Symbolism*, p. 46). As applicable to literary experience this confirms what should be obvious: given the centrality of the reader, conformation is how literary texts mean. The aesthetic efficacy of literature that is read as such (for its own sake and not, say, as an illustration of critical theory) thus resides in its ability to determine literary experience in the making, something that is linked, obviously enough, on each occasion of reading to the background, orientation, and ability of the reader.

It would be reductive, however, to think of literary experience strictly in terms of causal efficacy (epistemologically, the "primitive obviousness of the perception of 'conformation' "). Nor would it be adequate to regard it simply as vivid presentational impressions that relegate "information as to the past or the future" (*Process and Reality*, p. 168) to nonliterary, or to what Stein Haugom Olsen calls "information," discourse. The epistemology of literary experience is more complex than pure presentational immediacy in Whitehead's sense. It is (to reiterate) a mixed mode of perception where a patterned, or thematic, interplay of presentational and causal phenomena are the bottom line, epistemologically speaking, of the literary aesthetic. The tag *presentational immediacy of literary experience* does not refer, as does Whitehead's notion of pure presentational immediacy, to the apprehension of presentational data in abstraction from their dramatic impact (without which literary experience as participatory engagement is inconceivable). The dramatic power of literature attests to causal efficacy as a principle of cohesion in the very structure and evolution of literary meaning. The drama of literary experience—in which perception is the epistemic form of judgment—is a nexus of causal efficacy and the presentationally immediate, whereby the vivacity of presentational awareness both articulates and amplifies extended and evolving ideas (i.e., themes) through sensuously concrete (although not always sensuous) description and depiction.

Whitehead suggests this identification of the dramatic component of awareness with the perception of causal efficacy when he observes in

Symbolism that "the deep significance disclosed by Causal Efficacy is at the roots of the pathos which haunts the world" (p. 47). To illustrate his meaning Whitehead turns to literary experience (revealing his well-known love for, and affinity with, the English Romantics):

> The final stanza of Keats' "Eve of St. Agnes" commences with the haunting lines:
> "And they are gone: ay, ages long ago
> Those lovers fled away into the storm."
> There the pathos of the lapse of time arises from the imagined fusion of the perceptive modes by one intensity of emotion. (Pp. 47–48)

Whitehead is primarily concerned here with elements of awareness whose interaction (in a "mixed mode of perception") nearly all of human experience illustrates.[38] As such, his comment might appear somewhat lame from the specialized standpoint of literary criticism. Where the aim is to expound upon specifically literary experience, however, the impact of the pathos Keats's lines generate is the beginning of, and indeed the justification for, analysis. With a compelling if melodramatic depiction of the medieval past serving as the ambient of the lovers' flight, the "one intensity of emotion" to which Whitehead alludes arises from a form of perception involving the interaction of two pure perceptual modes. Whitehead uses the term *symbolic reference* to refer to the interrelation between presentational immediacy and causal efficacy—one class of which I take to be the epistemological deep-structure of the presentational immediacy of literary experience, and as such the starting point for literary analysis. In this recognition that the interconnection of the two modes of perception is the basis of symbolism, Whitehead confirms a key assumption of the present study: namely, that literary experience is a symbolic form.[39] This presupposition underlies my contention that literary meaning owes its form to the epistemological structure of the literary aesthetic, by which I mean the presentational immediacy of literary experience.

Literary experience involves a species of symbolic reference in which the deliverances of perception assume a presentational rather than a causal cast: the concern is with form, not formulation, with the aesthetic as opposed to the discursive. Nevertheless, perception that evidences causal efficacy is a sine qua non of coherent experience, and such perception is vividly operative in the presentational immediacy of literary experience. In fact, the causal efficacy that is tacitly apprehended as we read literature might be called the "principle of vividness" in literary experience and is manifest in the "direct experience of literature" (*The Educated Imagina-*

tion, p. 21). While in literary experience then the formulation of a mythos (literary thematic development) is not perceived as a conceptual "structuration" (Ricoeur's barbarization), it is experienced in the felt value—in the dramatic intensities—of what is described and depicted in literary art. The form, the coherence, that the perception of literary experience assumes is thematic.[40] Themes are the seminal perceptual factor of literary experience, just as they are, for example, in musical experience. Words or sounds that do not intelligibly describe or depict thought or sentiment (either in themselves or in a larger frame of reference in which they are embedded) are incapable of generating literary or musical experience.

Consider, for instance, the theme of the Chautauqua in Robert M. Pirsig's *Zen and the Art of Motorcycle Maintenance*.[41] As the narrator puts it, a Chautauqua is

> an old-time series of popular talks intended to edify and entertain, improve the mind and bring culture and enlightenment to the ears and thoughts of the hearers. (P. 7)

The various topics of the Chautauqua—ranging from the contrast between "classic" and "romantic" understanding to the philosophy of science to the theory of rhetoric—are in themselves hardly the stuff of literary experience. Nevertheless, they are not as patently digressive in the context of Pirsig's narrative as, say, "The Town-Ho's Story" is in *Moby-Dick*. Pirsig's discussions at least depict the narrator's thought processes, depiction that expresses and amplifies the theme of a psychically devastating pursuit of qualitative over quantitative standards of valuation.

The Chautauqua is a component of what might be called a narrative of "therapeutic remembering."[42] Remembering, recollection, is the principal dynamic of storytelling. And while a good deal of the content of the Chautauqua has nothing to do with remembering, the historical and theoretical discussion interwoven throughout the story is dialectically integrated with the narrative of the motorcycle vacation trip. The interrelation of the frame story and the Chautauqua is overt in passages such as the following:

> I've decided today's Chautauqua [the narrator uses the term in referring both to individual discussions and to the entire series] will begin to explore Phaedrus' world. It was intended earlier simply to restate some of his ideas that relate to technology and human values and make no reference to him personally, but the pattern of thought and memory that occurred last night has indicated this is not the

way to go. To omit him now would be to run from something that should not be run from. (P. 63)[43]

The Chautauqua evolves in consonance with and dramatically amplifies the events of the frame story. Although it has been categorized as non-fiction, *Zen* is a complex and powerful narrative—a psychodrama that owes much of its affective impact to the thematic of the Chautauqua, which subserves the leitmotif of therapeutic remembering. The role of the Chautauqua in Pirsig's novel thus exemplifies the function of theme as a dramatic component in literary experience generally, where narrative —storytelling, fabling—unifies conceptual and emotive dimensions of awareness.

The unified character of the literary aesthetic is evidenced by the presentational immediacy of literary experience. The type of cognitive apprehension that students of human experience conceive as resulting in the qualitative immediacy that marks presentational awareness is *intuition*. A look at the notion of intuition as it is relevant to literary experience completes the necessarily abbreviated inquiry into the epistemology of literary experience undertaken in this chapter. Ranging as it does from the phenomenology of the content of literary experience to the epistemic process that realizes that experience, this second section outlines a comprehensive and, as chapter 3 aims to show, an appropriate theoretical frame of reference for construing literary metaphor as a depictive image.

As the primitive epistemological modality, the way, at bottom, literature is taken as an actual presentation of reality (and not as an interpretation or a perspective), intuition is the first principle of a phenomenological analysis of literary experience. Edmund Husserl is clear about the primary status of intuition in experience. In his classic *Ideas*, he describes intuition as the fundamental kind of awareness and the root and purpose of rational discourse:

> Immediate "seeing" (*Sehen*), not merely sensory seeing, but *seeing in general as primordial dator* ["Object-giving"] *consciousness of any kind whatsoever*, is the ultimate source of justification for all rational statements. (P. 76)

Husserl thus considers intuition the

> *principle of all principles: that very primordial dator Intuition is a source of authority (Rechtsquelle) for knowledge, that whatever presents itself in "intuition" in primordial*

form (as it were in its bodily reality [i.e., in its sensuous immediacy]), *is simply to be accepted as it gives itself out to be,* though *only within the limits in which it then presents itself.* (P. 83)

Husserl's position on the primordiality of intuition suggests that as a prediscursive, aesthetically immediate mode of consciousness, literary experience is in the final analysis to be appreciated for what it is, and not in the reduced form of derivative, abstract (linguistic or other specialized) concepts nor in terms of their frames of meaning. This does not, however, in any way impugn the legitimacy of other kinds of knowing in the *explication* and *enhancement* of literary experience. Although the data of literary experience are "to be accepted" as authentic literary intuitions only in their prediscursive immediacy, they have no intrinsically privileged status vis-à-vis other sorts of data in other contexts. From the perspective, for example, of a psychological interpretation of Henry James's *The Ambassadors,* Strether's recollection of the personal tragedies of his early years may be an important factor in the reader's literary experience insofar as it helps to make intelligible a psychosocial "crisis of generativity"[44] at the heart of the narrative. On the other hand, in a reading orchestrated by, say, the idea of James's handling of the "international" theme, Strether's recollection may have little bearing on the literary experience of the story.

In the opening chapter of *Aesthetic as Science of Expression and General Linguistic,* Benedetto Croce brilliantly discerns the efficacy of the integral unity of intuition, asserting that the "whole [of aesthetic intuition] is that which determines the quality of the parts" (p. 2). This observation is itself a product of analytic thought, and it must be borne in mind that as the *intuitive* apprehension of meaning literary experience is not composed of "parts" in the same sense as are physical or conceptual constructs. The whole of a literary experience through any given point in a reading determines the (dramatic) quality of the presentational immediacy of literary experience at that point. To analyze and slice up experience into parts or elements is to employ discursive reason, what Croce refers to as "logical knowledge." This kind of cognizing is the application of concepts in order to establish or formulate one or more perspectives on experience, points of view that are products of contexts of awareness *extrinsic* to the experience submitted to analysis. (The problem of the "whole" and the "part" will be taken up again in connection with the "hermeneutic circle," in chapter 3, section 5.) This is not to suggest that the intuition of aesthetic experience in general and that of literary experience in particular are without ideational content.[45] On the contrary, "A work of art," as Croce explains,

> may be full of philosophical concepts; it may contain them in greater abundance and they may there be even more profound than in a philosophical dissertation, which in its turn may be rich to overflowing with descriptions and intuitions. But notwithstanding all these concepts the total effect of the work of art is an intuition; and notwithstanding all those intuitions, the total effect of the philosophical dissertation is a concept. (Pp. 2–3)

Although Croce uses intuition in a more general and objectivist sense than is necessary or even defensible for referring to the fundamental epistemological modality of literary experience, his perception of the often profound conceptual content of intuitive awareness is hardly a matter of dispute and is particularly apropos of literary experience.

Given that works of art concern and develop abstract ideas, questions arise about the status of the concepts that intuitive experience communicates. If, for instance, a literary work like *Zen and the Art of Motorcycle Maintenance* is replete with philosophical ideas that at various points get elaborated and analyzed at some length, how can reading the novel be a literary experience? A Crocean answer to questions of this sort is that, when the ideational content of a work of art is apprehended in the context of the work as a whole, the conceptual data are no longer abstractions of thought but become part of intuitive experience. Croce maintains that

> concepts which are found mingled and fused with . . . intuitions are no longer concepts, in so far as they are mingled and fused, for they have lost all independence and autonomy. (P. 2)

Croce is not alone on this point. Sartre in "The Role of Image in the Mental Life" holds a similar view, citing with approbation the following statement by A. Flach:

> In symbolic schemes a thought is always grasped, due to the fact that the conceptual relations that constitute it are lived intuitively. . . . (In *Essays in Existentialism*, p. 262)

As part of the symbolic scheme of *Zen and the Art of Motorcycle Maintenance*, the Chautauqua, insofar as it contributes to the drama of the narrator's story about himself (that is, to the degree that it enriches, indeed, *is an element of* literary experience), is, epistemically speaking, isomorphic with the impressions Pirsig conveys in the depictions of natural scenery, the interrelationship between the characters, and the psychic conflict associated with Phaedrus, the narrator's former self. The claim made earlier that the Chautauqua evolves in consonance with and dramatically amplifies the events of the frame story can thus be substantiated on epistemological grounds: the two types of meaning (the presentationally immediate and the abstractly conceptual) that appear to interrelate dialectically are present and of a piece qualitatively in the dramatic matrix of literary experience. They are known—or better, "lived"—in the same way: intuitively. As Cassirer observed, art and the artist

> do not live in a world of concepts, nor do they live in a world of sense-perceptions. They have a realm of their own. . . . It is a world not of concepts, but of intuition. . . . (*Symbol, Myth, and Culture*, p. 86)

That most intuitively minded of philosophers, George Santayana, considered intuition "the most intense form of existence," as "actuality or existence concentrated into the sense of existence."[46] In terms of the literary aesthetic this "sense of existence" is the drama of the presentational immediacy of literary experience. The dramatic intensity of literary experience and of aesthetic perception in general is not merely passive enjoyment but, like any engaging stage play, participative activity. This view that aesthetic perception and perception generally are participative activities is widely held[47] and hardly restricted to speculative philosophy.

The participative dimension of literary experience—what might be called "enactive envisagement"—is actually performative, and hence pervasively dramatic.[48] It corresponds in significant measure to what Frye refers to in *Anatomy of Criticism* as "internal mimesis": an "inward representation of sound and imagery" (p. 250). The correspondence between the perceptual participation of literary experience and Frye's "internal mimesis" is inexact, however, because literary experience is *not an imitation* of anything,[49] nor does it involve the imaginative re-presentation of some ideal literary image or meaning. Both of these latter views presuppose a subject-object dichotomy that supervenes upon the immediacy of intuitive experience.[50] Whitehead's comment on the limits of modern philosophical thought resulting from this sort of dichotomizing is relevant in this connection:

> All modern philosophy hinges round the difficulty of describing the world in terms of subject and object, substance and quality, particular and universal. The result always does violence to that immediate experience which we express in our actions,

our hopes, our sympathies, our purposes, and which we enjoy in spite of our lack of phrases for its verbal analysis. (*Process and Reality*, pp. 49–50)

Literary experience is holistic reading: no narrative or conceptual *ding an sich* gets articulated in consciousness via literary reading. It is a communicative occasion par excellence in which the receiver of the message (or vision) self-referentially performs the role of the sender (and in so doing complements the sender's overt or tacit performance of the role of receiver). The participative aspect of literary experience thus comes near to what mimesis signified in its earliest pre-Platonic acceptation: an hieratic, Dionysian (i.e., ecstatic) performance of dancing, music, and song.[51] The mimesis of literary experience is dramatic, per-formative in the original sense, and as such "thoroughly completes" the literary artist's communicative effort.[52] Literary experience is thus an actual communing, a collaboration with the creator that is on the order of ritual. And the mimesis of literary experience ultimately serves the same function that Susanne Langer discerns in the mimesis of cultic rite:[53]

to influence [in the case of literary art, human] nature, to formulate ideas [objectified in the drama of presentational awareness], to unite people with each other and with all spirits in their ambient in primitive communion, and to assure them of the power of their superlative asset, their humanity, their Mind. (*Mind*, vol. 3, p. 62)

Literary experience and hence the reading of literature has a consecration of its own. Hardly an imaginative copying or imitating, reading, as Maurice Blanchot has said, is a creative act: "more creative" than "creation"—"although it produces nothing." Blanchot's inspired thoughts on literary reading aptly frame, and so provide a fitting point of closure, for the foregoing exposition of literary experience:

Reading is not a conversation, it neither discusses nor questions. It never asks the book, let alone the author: "What exactly did you want to say? What truth do you impart?" An authentic reading never challenges the authentic book. But neither is it a total surrender to the "text." Only the non-literary book is obviously [self-evidently] a solid system of definite meanings, a complex of true statements. . . . the book whose origin is in art has no sponsors in the world and when it is read it has never been read before and achieves its reality as a book only in the space [or, in the terminology of the present study, the presentational immediacy] this single reading creates, every time for the first time. (*Sirens' Song*, p. 252)

3. Summary

The opening chapter concluded by asking where analysis of the meaning of metaphorical meaning ought to begin. The present chapter offers one way of answering that question with respect to literary metaphor. While the phenomenological approach to literary experience detailed in the preceding two sections is rooted in the thought of a major school of contemporary philosophy, some of the concepts and formulations, such as the *presentational immediacy of literary experience* and the *mimesis of literary experience*, are notions that, so far as I know, have not been explicated elsewhere.

Literary experience is characterized in this chapter as an organically unified, processive mode of aesthetic perception. The content of awareness in literary reading is seen as charged with the vivid immediacy and affective veracity of perceptual fact—anything less is a lapse of attention or a turning from literary experience to analytic (deliberative as opposed to perceptual) construal. More than a form of awareness in which a reader passively receives impressions of various sorts, literary experience is as active and transformative as perception itself. Although it is prediscursive and intuitive, literary experience is, like perception, selective and synthetic in a way that suggests analytic categories and operations, distinctions and modes of construal that critical discursive thinking explicitly formulates (and for that reason is generally understood to constitute).

Literary experience is active, performative, involving conformation with the text to the degree that the text influences the literary reader's way of apprehending meaning so as to "narrativize" (dramatically to charge, as it were) conscious awareness. Conformity of this sort demonstrably contributes to literary experience insofar as the evolution of ideas or themes demonstrably present in the text engenders a correlative evolution of presentational data in the reader's awareness.[54]

Literary experience, like aesthetic apprehension in general, is perceptual rather than conceptual, as Cassirer concluded: "In art we do not conceptualize the world, we perceptualize it" (*Symbol, Myth, and Culture*, p. 186). The issue of how, phenomenologically, the world of a poem, novel, or other type of literary art is "perceptualized" is addressed in this chapter in terms of what I call the presentational immediacy of literary experience. Experientially speaking, the content of perception is what is immediately present for awareness. The "what" is not purely objective nor is it an unmediated product of fancy. The phenomenological content of perceptual awareness consists of what Cassirer termed "intuitive symbols" (*Symbol, Myth, and Culture*, p. 186). The reader in the process of literary reading is not apprehending "a language of verbal symbols," at least to the extent that he is apprehending language as a vehicle of intuitive symbols, as a means, that is, of communicating aesthetic form.[55] For it is through intuitive symbols that the reader participates firsthand (in terms of presentationally immediate descriptions and depictions) in a "process of vision"—such as that which Henry James explains in the preface to *The Ambassadors* that it is his purpose to "demonstrate" in the novel. But far more than the evolving moral and aesthetic consciousness of Louis Lambert Strether, the process of vision to which James refers suggests participation in the vital world, or world version, that unfolds in all worthwhile literature. Phenomenologically speaking, every work of literary art demonstrates to the literary reader a process of vision. Yet in literary experience more occurs: the reader actually participates in this demonstration, so that what to the analytic eye is a narratively rendered perspective on human situations and events is for the reader-participator an occasion of envisioning. Perhaps the greatest value of literary studies is that they enable readers thus to envision—and in so doing to participate in—a rich and profound range of processes of seeing. Literature thereby stands to reveal and make accessible subtly nuanced and radically different imaginative domains from which to value the drama of human experience.

To assert that through presentationally immediate descriptions and depictions the literary reader participates in the process of vision that literary works articulate implies that, insofar as any discernible object is conceptually suggestive or emotively evocative in a given literary context, the suggestions or evocations are, for literary experience. *intrinsic* to that object. To abstract a literary-experiential entity—a color, an idea, a scene, a personality, or an action—from the feelings and thoughts it conveys and is associated with in its thematic context is to engage in something completely different than the enactive envisaging that is literary experience.

Since the data of reading acquire their meaning for literary experience only in their thematic context, it follows that what is presentationally manifest in literary experience is thematically disposed. The thematic disposition of what is presentationally immediate in literary reading is experienced phenomenologically as drama. The awareness of drama, which in the unity of aesthetic perception becomes the drama of awareness, is an index of a reader's evaluation or judgment and is inherent in the very perception of the evolving image, scene, or vision that is presentationally immediate at any point in literary reading.

The wholeness or coherence of what is presentationally immediate is not a matter of causal chains of events or of themes abstractly considered. It is the consciousness of drama—more specifically, of a thematically structured dramatic figuration that operates as the principle of coherence and unity in the dynamic, ever-evolving present of literary experience. This dramatic moment (involving, as it does, the reader's collaborative conformation) constitutes the unity of the literary aesthetic and is the way that the thematic and (as themes are ramified concepts) the conceptual content of a literary work manifests itself in presentational awareness.

Literary experience is a symbolic form and is as such a mode of what Cassirer identifies as mythical consciousness: "a world" that is not structured by "natural powers that may be reduced to certain causal [or rhetorical or linguistic or semiotic] laws but a dramatic world" (*Symbol, Myth, and Culture*, p. 172). The philosopher of symbolic forms perceived that such a world—a world that generates and sustains literature—is not bounded by spatial, temporal, or physical determinations: "Nothing has a definite and permanent shape; everything is liable to sudden transformations and transfigurations" (p. 174).[56] Such is the magic of the human imagination and such the fertile ground of metaphor in literary experience. As Ralph Waldo Emerson brilliantly observes in his essay "The Poet":

> the quality of the imagination is to flow, and not to freeze. The poet did not stop at the color, or the form, but read their meaning, neither may he rest in his meaning, but makes the same objects experiments of his new thought. . . . For all symbols are fluxional; all language is vehicular and transitive. . . . (*Collected Works*, vol. 3, p. 20)[57]

With a phenomenological account of literary experience in place we turn next to how literary metaphor means. The view detailed in the chapter that follows takes its bearings from this second section of the study. Its claim to originality is more a matter of emphasis and adequacy with respect to literary experience than of startlingly novel insights or subtle formulations. Chapter 3 introduces a phenomenological approach to literary metaphor and explicates metaphor as a depictive image. The meaning of metaphorical imagery and depiction developed in what follows is elaborated in terms of the presuppositions and conceptualizations of the foregoing phenomenological analysis of literary experience.

In connection with the analysis of the literary image and of metaphor as depictive image, I consider the place of discursive, analytic thinking in a practicable experiential view of metaphor. This is hardly digressive since it addresses issues that arise concerning the construal of metaphor in the explication of literary texts. An inquiry into the limits of analysis vis-à-vis literary experience leads to a pluralism in light of which the most appropriate analytic strategy in the explication of literary metaphor is the one that on any given occasion most enhances the literary experience of a particular reader.[58] The question of which analytic schema or interpretive tack is "true" or most correct for a given literary text (and hence which occasions of reading and which readers contribute, on the other hand, to "freakish" literary experience) remains what in fact it always has been: a matter of judgment based on various personal, professional, and specialized priorities—a matter of interpretive politics. It does not as such call for definitive treatment in a study concerned with the phenomenology of aesthetic perception, one focused, that is, on the qualitative dimension of perspective in general and for its own sake.

CHAPTER THREE

Literary Metaphor

THE DEPICTIVE IMAGE

Here in the centre stands the glass, Light
Is the lion that comes down to drink. There
And in that state, the glass is a pool.
Ruddy are his eyes and ruddy are his claws
When light comes down to wet his frothy jaws.

WALLACE STEVENS
"The Glass of Water"

. . . poetry is story.

MARK VAN DOREN
The Happy Critic

Having examined the major approaches to metaphor in the opening chapter and having articulated, in the second, a phenomenological literary aesthetic as the ground, or metalanguage, of discourse about literary metaphor, we can turn to how literary metaphor means—how it operates, that is, in literary experience. The present chapter expands upon the notion of literary metaphor as a depictive image and argues that metaphorical depiction, conceived in the context of literary experience, affords significant insight into how metaphor functions in literary art.

The sections that follow (1) find literary metaphor integrated within frames of meaning on the level of discourse (the position of Paul Ricoeur in *The Rule of Metaphor*; see especially studies 7 and 8)—the level of thematic development—rather than on the level of the word, phrase, or sentence; (2) hold that it conveys meaning depictively, that is, prediscursively, antepredicatively; and (3) conceive literary metaphor as a field phenomenon that operates holographically: each characteristic of the image implicating the entire literary thematic context that occasions the metaphorical figure. The view of literary metaphor argued for in this chapter is not vitiated by theoretical difficulties in the explication of metaphor arising from the problematic dichotomy between a vehicle or focus and its tenor or frame (Richards, Black), nor from the dubious ontology of "tension" between alternative meanings (Foss, Wheelwright, Berggren, et al.), nor from some occult mechanism of semantic transfer (Aristotle, Levin, Hrushovski, Gumpel, et al.).

Before taking up metaphoric depiction, we need to be clear about the meaning of *image* in "depictive image." As with most terms that designate phenomena analyzed in diverse disciplines, *image* has many and widely varied connotations. The phenomenological and, more specifically, the literary experiential orientation of the present study calls for an understanding of the concept that is both true to the phenomenology of literary experience and consistent with the function of metaphor.

1. *The Literary Image*

In *Disenchanted Images: A Literary Iconology* Theodore Ziolkowski reviews the most commonly held conceptions of the literary image.[1] Ziolkowski explains that in literary studies "image" usually designates "at least three separate phenomena": icons, or "things with a tangible reality in the context of the literary work" (p. 8); rhetorical figures (metaphor, simile, and other tropes); and mental images. He charges that the notions of literary imagery that derive from the second and third senses are problematic for a number of reasons. Citing an objection raised by the German scholar Hermann Pongs, Ziolkowski argues that to identify literary imagery with a rhetorical figure such as metaphor is incorrect, since " 'image' is hardly a synonym for 'metaphor' because a picture is not a comparison, an icon is not an analogy." Ziolkowski further differentiates metaphor from the image when he asserts (still referring to Pongs's analysis) that "metaphor attempts to illuminate the essence of things by exposing previously unrecognized analogies, whereas the image aims at rendering visible iconically" (p. 10).

The contention that a picture and an icon are different from a comparison and an analogy is hardly disputable, and by eschewing the reductive construal of literary image as a mere rhetorical figure, Ziolkowski's observation is faithful to the character of literary experience. Two fundamental objections nevertheless can be raised against Ziolkowski's bifurcation of metaphor and image. The first objection has to do with the designation of the image as a phenomenon that is in some sense visible, as a picture or an icon. It is just not the case that all literary imagery is picturable, as this opening couplet from a well-known poem by e. e. cummings makes plain:

> my father moved through dooms of love
> through sames of am through haves of give . . .
>
> (*50 Poems*, p. 34)

The powerful existential-psychological imagery of these lines defies visualization, whether of the imitative or the mirroring variety.[2] The second objection to Ziolkowski's designation of metaphor as something other than an image concerns his assumption that metaphor is merely a rhetorical trope that compares or analogizes: views based on such assumptions prove flawed on close analysis. (See section 1 of chapter 1 for an explication and critique of comparison and analogy theories of metaphor.)

Citing Norman Friedman's entry "Imagery" in the *Princeton Encyclopedia of Poetry and Poetics*, Ziolkowski explains that the notion of the mental image, the third of the three ways that literary images are commonly conceived,

> borrowed from psychology and deriving originally from Hobbes, refers to 'the reproduction in the mind of a sensation produced by a physical perception': notably visual, auditory, olfactory, gustatory, tactile, organic, and kinesthetic. (P. 9)

Ziolkowski finds the classification of literary imagery as mental imagery in this sense unsatisfactory on the grounds that literary images elicit various and frequently contrasting impressions in different readers, so that no literary image could be definitively fixed as, say, visual or tactile. He goes on to cast this objection in terms of the activity of literary interpretation:

> mental imagery helps very little in our understanding of the literary work because the reader must inevitably supply the response, the impression that is in his own mind. What strikes one reader as a tactile image may seem primarily visual to another (e.g., rain or ice or glowing metal). As Furbank puts it [in *Reflections on the Word "Image"* (London, 1970)] "mental images are what you tell yourself they are." Moreover Norman Friedman points out that "in focusing upon the sensory qualities of images themselves, it diverts attention from the *function* of those images in the poetic context." (P. 10)

Ziolkowski's citation of Friedman's statement in this passage is crucial. Without doubt, the abstraction of literary imagery from its context promotes the simplistic view of literary experience as a parade of isolable, static mental images amenable to definitive examination in the same way as are slices of once-living tissue on a slide. An important factor of literary imagery that Ziolkowski fails to mention in this connection, however, is the architectonic significance of the literary image conceived as a mental event. The literary contexts that occasion imagery are amplified by that same imagery. Conversely, the contextual reach of literary imagery is part of its definition (and characteristic of it as a field phenomenon). Thus, besides being variably significant from reader to reader, the literary image is not strictly bounded by the imagistic term, or what I refer to as the *center* of a literary image. Consider this opening couplet of a familiar poem by Emily Dickinson:

> "Hope" is the thing with feathers—
> That perches in the soul—
> (*Complete Poems*, p. 116)

To regard the limits of the metaphoric image "thing with feathers" as just three words exclusive of the contextually salient imagistic characterization of the second line would be no less arbitrary than to contend that the image consists solely of "thing."

Ziolkowski favors the first of the three "phenomena" that he cites—the icon—as the most accurate way to conceive of the literary image. Archetypally, images are, in his view,

> representations of a person in the form of statues or optical reflections. . . . these *literal* images also happen to be *literary* images in the primary critical sense of the word—that is, the iconic representation of concrete objects that are depicted as having physical presence in the work itself. (P. 11)

By maintaining that literary imagery is iconic and by assimilating "literal" to "*literary* images in the primary critical sense of the word," Ziolkowski betrays an objectivist bias, for he fails to distinguish the actually visual, auditory, tactile, etc., from the imaginatively pictured, heard, or touched in his definition of iconic representation.

A key difficulty with views such as Ziolkowski's is rooted in the tendentiously visual sense in which they characterize "depiction" and in the way literary images are understood to "depict." The experiential meaning of the depiction that literary images effect can hardly be determined satisfactorily without appeal to a cogent and comprehensive account of literary experience, the medium of literary imagistic depiction. On the basis of the phenomenological aesthetic of literary experience detailed in the preceding chapter, *literary depiction* can be understood as the way in which imagery "narrativizes" articulated literary themes by rendering them presentational, aesthetically immediate. Ziolkowski uncritically abstracts from (and so ends up misconstruing) literary experience when he states that literary images are representations "of concrete objects that are depicted as having physical presence in the work itself" (p. 11). This implies that although images are elements of depiction they are not instrumental to—the means of—depiction. For to hold that the image is a *representation* of an object that *gets depicted* as having a physical presence in a literary work is not the same thing as to maintain that it is the actual *means of* depiction, which implies recognizing the image as the actual embodiment of meaning in presentational awareness rather than as an instance of mimesis in the commonly accepted and problematic sense.

Perhaps the most significant weakness of Ziolkowski's formulation becomes apparent when we ask what it means to say that something is depicted *as having physical presence* in a literary work when the concept of depiction is divorced from that of representation. The theoretical difficulty that this question indicates is obviated if we conceive literary depiction as the dynamic of presentational immediacy of literary experience. Edward S. Casey is more faithful here to the phenomenological facts of imagistic depiction in literary experience when he defines image functionally, as "the *manner* of presentation, that is the specific way in which an imagined content and the imaginal margin [the indistinct outer fringe of that content] are together given to the imaginer's consciousness" (*Imagining*, p. 56).

Depiction is a cardinal notion in the theory of literary metaphor presented in this study, and I shall consider it in more detail in section 3, which focuses explicitly on the topic of literary metaphor. The point to stress here is that literary images are not necessarily picturable[3] and that they are not isolable as representations of objects that get instantiated through depiction in literary texts. Rather, they are a mode of the aesthetic articulation of meaning—a symbolic form—employed for the purposes of description and depiction (the distinction between which is delineated in section 3). Invoking the "aesthetic articulation of meaning" in explaining depiction adumbrates the shift to a determinately phenomenological approach to the literary image, the principal theoretical orientation of this inquiry. Phenomenological analysis affords an experientially grounded perspective on the literary image and further elaborates the theory of literary experience outlined in chapter 2 by revealing how the literary image is a component of literary experience. In doing so it provides a rationale for the view argued in section 3 that, as a constitutive phenomenon of literary experience, literary metaphor is a *depictive* image.

In his *Psychology of Imagination* Jean-Paul Sartre undertakes a penetrating phenomenological investigation of the image.[4] Probing the way that imagery functions in consciousness by examining a number of seminal relationships between imagery, intuition, and understanding, Sartre begins his discussion of the symbol with an observation that corroborates the contention that in literary experience the image as a representation of an object is not isolable as such from a matrix of presentational meaning (in Sartre's terms, "thought"). "The image," writes Sartre, "serves neither as illustration nor as support for thought. It is in no way different from thought" (in *Existentialism*, p. 257).

Further on, Sartre offers a phenomenological explanation of the image that distinguishes between analytic and prediscursive spheres of awareness, an explanation that suggests the place of imagery in the presentational immediacy of literary experience:

> What we ordinarily designate as *thinking* is a consciousness which affirms this or that of its objects but without realizing the qualities on [*sic*] the object. The *image*, on the contrary, is a consciousness that aims to produce its object: it is therefore constituted by a certain way of judgment and feeling of which we do not become conscious as such but which we apprehend *on* the intentional object as this or that of its qualities. In a word: the function of the image is *symbolic*. (P. 258)

This passage makes explicit a fundamental assumption of the phenomenological perspective on literary experience articulated in the present study, namely, that the conscious realization of qualitative experience—aesthetic perception—is a function of primary, or "first-order," awareness (as opposed to analytic self-awareness, the critical consciousness of consciousness). In distinguishing self-reflective analytic thinking from imagistic experience by categorizing the former as "a consciousness which affirms," Sartre has a precedent in Sir Philip Sidney, whose famous declaration that "the Poet, he nothing affirmeth" clearly anticipates Sartre's epistemological assumptions.

Sartre's reference to "a certain way of judgment and feeling of which we do not become conscious as such" could serve as a definition of the pre-discursive mode of awareness peculiar to literary experience. As operative on that plane of consciousness, the literary image is in fact "constituted by" literary experience, the intelligibility of which is manifested in its presentational character. Conversely, literary experience is the symbolic form in the context of which the literary image realizes its symbolic function. Literary images are thus composed of the epistemological stuff of the meaning that they communicate (and in that sense only are they literal).

When he turns to the intuitive basis of the apprehension of imagery, Sartre relies heavily on the work of A. Flach, whom he quotes at considerable length. Flach's insights help to clarify how the literary image operates as what Cassirer called an "intuitive symbol," and they suggest phenomenologically how literary imagery communicates concepts (that, as articulated in literary art, are what I refer to as themes) on a prediscursive level of awareness: that of the presentational immediacy of literary experience. Flach maintains that

> In symbolic schemes a thought is always grasped, due to the fact that the conceptual relations that constitute it are lived intuitively. . . . [the] intuitive image [and here Flach refers specifically to metaphor] expresses nothing else than a system of conceptual relationships which are grasped while the subject sees them as determined relationships between sensory data. (In *Existentialism*, p. 262)

For literary experience, "lived intuitively" translates as "apprehended presentationally"; and as the vehicle of the presentational communication of concepts linked in "story" (as themes), the literary image functions as a medium of authentically lived experience. It is otiose perhaps to indicate that because it takes the form of first-order consciousness the noetic entertainment of concrete, sensuous experience is "authentic" living in the same sense as are the impressions of a vivid dream or a hallucination (as opposed to a report or explanation of some phenomenon). Such a charge, however, can hardly apply to the contention that the apprehension of concepts imagistically depicted—and thus conveyed prediscursively, ante-predicatively—bears witness to the way literary art renders ideas an authentic part of our phenomenological life. It is in this way, I submit, that literary images naturalize ideal experience in the reader's "life-world." According to Flach, this function of imparting concepts and conceptual relationships "live," as it were, is the sole purpose of the image as an expressive term. Granting this and assuming with thinkers such as

C. I. Lewis that the reference of expressive statements is ultimately the phenomenal, it seems clear that determining the function, the pragmatics, of the literary image involves inquiring into the presentational immediacy of literary experience, a phenomenological mode of awareness. In an explanation of how ideas can develop exclusive of deliberative consciousness, Sartre links the notion that imagery communicates conceptual relationships through depicting "determined relationships between sensory data" to that of presentational awareness:

> ideation can operate on the non-reflective plane: all that is needed is that the pure knowledge become debased into imaginative knowledge. . . . In that case, all thought becomes conscious of things including other thoughts and consciousness of itself. . . . This non-reflective plane may be called the *plane of presence* because of the attitude assumed by consciousness: it behaves as if it were *in the presence* of the object which it judges; that is to say, it seeks to apprehend that thing and to formulate ideas on it as an external object. (P. 272)

Despite Sartre's dubious Platonic stance on "pure knowledge" as somehow "debased" when rendered imagistically[5] and his vague assertion that presentational consciousness "seeks . . . to formulate ideas on" the image, he nevertheless perceives that imagery conveys ideas in the medium of presentational awareness. It is on the basis of this insight that Sartre's phenomenological analysis supports a seminal postulate of the present inquiry: that literary imagery, which includes literary metaphor, communicates ideas by means of thematically disposed imagistic (presentational) experience. As understood here, themes are concepts-become-narrative; when concepts get "told," mythicized, they orchestrate the literary imagery that functions as their prereflective, presentational vehicle of communication. Cassirer in the third volume of his *Philosophy of Symbolic Forms*[6] stresses the epistemic significance of intuitive, perceptual imagery in conveying abstract meaning presentationally, a capacity of the image that he suggestively labels "symbolic pregnance." Cassirer's lucid explication of the concept of symbolic pregnance is worth citing:

> the way in which perception [understood in the present study to include the noetic perception of literary imagery] as a sensory experience contains at the same time a certain nonintuitive meaning which it immediately and concretely represents. . . . the perception itself . . . by virtue of its own immanent organization, takes on a kind of spiritual articulation—which, being ordered in itself, also belongs to a

determinate order of meaning. In its full actuality, its living totality, it is at the same time a life "in" meaning. . . . this ideal interwovenness, this relatedness of the single perceptive phenomenon, given here and now, to a characteristic total meaning [is what Cassirer understands as the "pregnance" of a symbolic image]. (P. 202)

2. On the Function of Narrative Imagery in The Golden Bowl

An analysis of how literary imagery operates in a specific narrative context will illustrate how the approach to the image outlined in the preceding section applies practically to literary experience. A literary work replete with remarkable extended metaphorical imagery is Henry James's last completed novel, *The Golden Bowl*.[7] James employs the elaborate figurative language that pervades this subtly developed story to effect a number of narrative ends. In what follows, I focus on instances of two essential narrative components that James uses literary imagery both to express and to amplify: characterization and the evolution of consciousness. The imagery that contributes to the characterization of Adam Verver and that which depicts Maggie's coalescing sense of the adulterous collusion between her husband Amerigo and Charlotte, her young stepmother (who unknown to the Ververs is Amerigo's former lover), reveals two ways in which James masterfully employs the literary image for purposes of narrative development. More generally, an analysis of this sort helps to clarify how the literary image conveys abstract ideas wholly through the medium of prereflective, phenomenological experience.

James's use of vivid imagery attests to his keen appreciation of the narrative efficacy of dramatic exemplification. The brilliant chapel/forge figure early in the eighth chapter, for instance, depicts basic aspects of Adam Verver's character. The spirit of the "artlessly-artful" millionaire is dramatized as a "spark of fire, the point of light, [that] sat somewhere in his inward vagueness as a lamp before a shrine twinkles in the dark perspective of a church" (vol. 1, p. 127). The "dark perspective" is a suggestive objective correlative of Verver's "inward vagueness." As the metaphorical vignette develops, the image of the church metamorphoses into that of a forge: the "stiff American breeze" that for a certain period earlier in his life blew hard upon Verver's "inner spark" created a "chamber" that was the "workshop of fortune." By this retrospective characterization effected by the evolving literary image, James conveys with dramatic economy the inner development of his protagonist.

The unprecedented, miraculous "white-heat" of Adam Verver's cerebral temperature" during the years that he made his fortune is something that he himself—"the master of the forge"—"practically" feels unable to explain. As in a forge, where intense energy is harnessed through the discipline of rigorous application, the potent force of Verver's cerebral flame has been "extraordinarily contained." The forge image communicates in a vivid and concrete way the "kind of acquired power" James would have us apprehend that Adam Verver realized in his youth and early middle age. Later in the passage, Verver's cerebral flame is explained as his great "variety of imagination." The self-discipline that the forge image dramatizes and that tempers this personal asset enables him to succeed in a great way in "the world of affairs." A peculiar feature of Verver's profound self-possession (one that James exploits for both comic and dramatically ironic ends) is that it is "not to be distinguished from monotony." This explains why Verver's extreme reserve, his unassuming demeanor—the "soft looseness, so to say, of his temper and tone"—attest not to a monotonously benign sensibility but rather to one that is acutely perceptive yet under strict governance. [8]

In a later extended figure, James enhances further the reader's presentational sense of Adam Verver by metaphorically rendering what could be called the "conative scheme" of Verver's acquisition of insight into his own potential: how he established a "relation" with his own mind. The dramatic image articulately conveys Verver's effort to acquire knowledge and gain control of his "private house":

> He had knocked at the door of that essentially private house, and his call, in truth, had not been immediately answered; so that when, after waiting and coming back, he had at last got in, it was twirling his hat, as an embarrassed stranger, or, trying his keys, as a thief in the night. He had gained confidence only with time, but when he had taken real possession of the place it had been never again to come away. (Vol. 1, p. 149)

This *imag*inary vision of Adam Verver's spiritual maturation imparts a clear sense of his diffident although determined endeavor to achieve a fullness of self-possession. This most personal of accomplishments is the source of his deepest satisfaction:

> All of [Verver's] success represented, it must be allowed, his one principle of pride . . . The right ground for elation was difficulty mastered, and his difficulty—thanks to his modesty—had been to believe in his facility. (P. 149)

The inner discipline depicted through the dynamics of the chapel-cum-forge image is significantly amplified in this passage. The inner strength that enabled Verver to harness his imaginative vitality and realize his potential in the world of affairs is the source of his pride. This pride, however, attaches to the perception of "difficulty mastered," a difficulty not material but one of nerve: his need to believe in his "facility," his practical intelligence. In this light, Adam Verver regards his huge success in business as a test of, an adventure in, self-mastery. His greatness is thus evidenced not in his having made a fortune but rather in his having done so being incidental to a personal process of "immense development."

James dramatizes the fundamental simplicity of Adam Verver's nature through the figure of a

> small decent room, clean-swept and unencumbered with furniture, but drawing a particular advantage, as might presently be noted, from the outlook of a pair of ample and uncurtained windows. There was something in Adam Verver's eyes that both admitted the morning and the evening in unusual quantities. . . . (Vol. 1, p. 170)

This image depicts order and openness that although on a modest scale nevertheless suggest prodigious capacity.

The characterization of Adam Verver evolves cumulatively through extended images and depicts a man who a daughter like Maggie (interpreting, as she does, his devotion to her as dependence) could feel needs coddling. Through most of the narrative Maggie is blind to her father's virtues of intellectual integrity and quiet strength; nevertheless, she comes greatly to depend on them. And it is when she most relies on her father's personal greatness that she suddenly sees it for what it is.

Toward the close of the thirty-seventh chapter, Adam Verver subtly intimates to Maggie that he would remove to America with Charlotte in answer to suspicions that Maggie has obliquely evinced, suspicions of which he is clearly well aware. After reassuring her that he will not feel sacrificed to the exigencies of her marital security if prompted to make the trip,

> he seemed to plant or to square himself for a kind of assurance it had occurred to him he might as well treat her to, in default of other things. . . . (Vol. 2, p. 273)

The effect of his gesture is immediate and dramatic. Maggie is suddenly conscious of her father as he actually is—the culmination of what, with all the vivid intensity and symbolic pregnance of his imagery, James has made him in the reader's presentational awareness:

The "successful," beneficent person, the beautiful, bountiful, original, dauntlessly wilful great citizen. . . . His quietness . . . as always part of everything, of his success, his originality, his modesty, his exquisite public perversity, his inscrutable incalculable energy. . . . (Vol. 2, p. 273)

Perhaps the most striking of the metaphorical images through which James narrativizes (i.e., renders presentational the thematic articulation of) the dynamics of awareness are those with which he tells of Maggie's growing suspicion about the adultery. The images that dramatize the young woman's accruing sense of the situation are essential to the development of plot in *The Golden Bowl*. And a look at two of them, as further instances of how literary images convey conceptual meaning, reveals the close inter-relation of perception and event—indeed, the depiction of perception *as* event—in this most phenomenologically psychological of novels.

The centers of two extended metaphors that perhaps most dramatically portray Maggie's growing perception of both the fact and the emotional ramifications of Charlotte and Amerigo's infidelity are the "pagoda" and the "family coach." Tracing the developing of Maggie's awareness as James narratively renders it through these metaphors reveals how literary imagery dramatizes abstractions of theme (in the present case, concepts such as *deception* and *manipulation*) by articulating them in the "imminent organization" of vividly perceptible phenomena. In what could be re-garded as a union of mythos and logos, these literary images emerge as an intrinsic component in the organization of the plot.

In the opening paragraph of Book Second of *The Golden Bowl*, James presents the arresting pagoda vignette:

It was n't till many days had passed that the Princess began to accept the idea of having done, a little, something she was not always doing, or indeed that of having listened to any inward voice that spoke in a new tone. Yet these instinctive post-ponements of reflexion were the fruit, positively, of recognitions and perceptions already active; of the sense above all that she had made at a particular hour, made by the mere touch of her hand, a difference in the situation so long present to her as practically unattackable. This situation had been occupying for months and months the very centre of the garden of her life, but it had reared itself there like some strange tall tower of ivory, or perhaps rather some wonderful beautiful but outlandish pagoda, a structure plated with hard bright porcelain, coloured and figured and adorned at the overhanging eaves with silver bells that tinkled ever so charmingly when stirred by chance airs. She had walked round and round it—that was what she felt; she had carried on her existence in the space left her for circulation, a space that sometimes seemed ample and sometimes narrow: looking up all the while at the fair structure that spread itself so amply and rose so high, but never quite making out as yet where she might have entered had she wished. She had n't wished till now—such was the odd case; and what was doubtless equally odd besides was that though her raised eyes seemed to distinguish places that must serve from within, and especially far aloft, as apertures and outlooks, no door appeared to give access from her convenient garden level. The great decorated surface had remained consistently impenetrable and inscrutable. At present however, to her considering mind, it was as if she had ceased merely to circle and to scan the elevation, ceased so vaguely, so quite helplessly to stare and wonder: she had caught herself distinctly in the act of pausing, then in that of lingering, and finally in that of stepping unprecedentedly near. The thing might have been, by the distance at which it kept her, a Mahometan mosque, with which no base heretic could take a liberty; there so hung about it the vision of one's putting off one's shoes to enter and even verily of one's paying with one's life if found there as an interloper. She had n't certainly arrived at the conception of paying with her life for anything she might do; but it was nevertheless quite as if she had sounded with a tap or two one of the rare porcelain plates. She had knocked in short—though she could scarce have said whether for admission or for what; she had applied her hand to a cool smooth spot and had waited to see what would happen. Something *had* happened; it was as if a sound, at her touch, after a little, had come back to her from within; a sound sufficiently suggesting that her approach had been noted. (Pp. 3–4)

Maggie's consciousness of the "situation," disturbing intimations of which have been occupying her for months, has matured to a definite conviction. Her protected, almost cloistered, personal world is a "garden" in the midst of which she has witnessed the growth of "some strange tall tower of ivory, or perhaps rather some wonderful beautiful but outlandish pagoda." Maggie's consciousness of being artfully diverted from some fact of towering significance in the center of her life is graphically depicted by the "great decorated surface" of the pagoda, that looms as an "impenetrable and inscrutable" presence. She is sensitive to possible danger in attempting to breach mysterious boundaries in her own garden, boundaries of elaborate propriety that are concomitants of the pagoda. But as she ponders the curious, exclusionary circumstance in her life (dramatized in her walk around the pagoda), we are apprised that "She had n't certainly arrived at the conception of paying with her life for anything she might do." Presently we learn that with scarcely discriminated purpose Maggie has "knocked." Further, she is aware of having been perceived by the occupants of the pagoda as intent on penetrating its mystery: "it was as if a sound, at her touch, after a little, had come back to her from within; a sound sufficiently suggesting that her approach had been noted." Through imagistically rendering Charlotte's and Amerigo's piqued awareness in this way, James delicately introduces Maggie's detection of the mutual suspicion that grows to pervade much of the second part of the novel.

As her thought evolves, Maggie realizes that she is being "treated" by her husband and stepmother. She becomes increasingly cognizant of having been trapped and diverted by decorous manners and the requirements of high social form. (As the imagery depicts *Maggie's* conscious apprehension, it omits a thematically germane factor in Maggie's entrapment, one that colors the reader's presentational entertainment of that imagery: her single-minded devotion to her father.) Maggie can hardly be expected to violate the values of her social milieu, for these inform her very sensibility—her life has been a "rich garden." The only way she can see her way through the situation so as to preclude the shame of open scandal and the unacceptable pain that she feels it would cause her father is to separate the adulterers without violating the rarified tone of her interpersonal relations (something Maggie accomplishes by drawing on her father's strength).

On an evening when Amerigo is "away from her again," Maggie contemplates how as a couple Charlotte and Amerigo have served her and her father. "Taking the field" together (putatively to fulfill the social obligations of their respective "sposi"), Amerigo and Charlotte give the impression of living "always in harness." This metaphor introduces the vignette of the "family coach," the depictive image that dramatizes the process of Maggie's developing thoughts on the role that her husband and Charlotte have played in the social economy of the family. Maggie recalls that Charlotte was

"had in," as the servants always said of extra help, because they had thus suffered it to be pointed out to them that if their family coach lumbered and struck the fault was in its lacking its complement of wheels. (Vol. 2, p. 23)

The result of admitting Charlotte into the family, of adding the "fourth wheel," was that "Nothing had been, immediately, more manifest than the greater grace of the movement of the vehicle" (p. 23). Maggie ponders how, with Charlotte as the fourth member of the family group, "every strain had been lightened for herself. So far as *she* was one of the wheels she had but to keep her place." Maggie then realizes that she "felt no weight," and that in fact "she had scarce to turn round." Thus, as the image evolves, it communicates both Maggie's mounting suspicion and her feeling of not being in control. As Maggie stands before the fire, the complex visual and conative depictive medium of her unfolding *imag*inative thought process becomes a vehicle of insight:

> She might have been watching the family coach pass and noting that, somehow, Amerigo and Charlotte were pulling it while she and her father were not so much as pushing. They were seated inside together . . . the exertion was *all* with the others. (Pp. 23–24)

The extended metaphor narrativizes (casts as objectively presentational the evolution of) Maggie's realization that she is being taken for a ride. In addition to depicting her sense of having lost control to Amerigo and Charlotte, the figure of the family coach also dramatizes Maggie's instinctive response to the situation. The image resolves in an act of conscious decision, as Maggie sees

> herself at last, in the picture she was studying, suddenly jump from the coach; whereupon, frankly, with the wonder of her sight, her eyes opened wider and her heart stood still for a moment. (P. 24)

This second of the literary images exemplifying James's narrative rendering of the resolution of conscious apprehension subtly orchestrates the play of Maggie's memories, impressions, and thought processes in an evolving picture that begins as a simple trope dramatizing her thoughts. The image grows reified as a quasi-hallucinogenic "projected vision" for Maggie as she stands before the fire. As such, it is a concise, intuitively immediate vehicle that enables her consciously to contemplate and synthesize her impressions and to work out her thoughts. Ultimately the figure evanesces in Maggie's fateful resolution "to do things differently in respect to Amerigo and Charlotte" (p. 25).

The foregoing discussion illustrates how literary imagery is in Cassirer's sense symbolically pregnant, intrinsically interrelated with the "characteristic total meaning"—the mythos—of a narrative. Indeed, it is as a formal constituent of the development of literary themes that literary imagery figuratively articulates abstract thoughts and concepts, and in so doing conveys them with the presentational immediacy of perceptual experience.

We turn, next, to how metaphorical literary imagery expresses ide-

ational meaning. The section that follows thus marks the convergence of
the two principal topics of this study: metaphor and literary experience.

3. *The Depictive Image*

At the most general level, all literary imagery articulates patterns of
relationships in presentational ways. The "family coach" in *The Golden
Bowl*, for instance, invokes both the material patterns characteristic of a
horse-drawn coach and those of the tensions involved in its support and
locomotion on three and then four wheels.[9] As metaphor in the context
of the narrative, the figure functions thematically (although, except in
analyses such as the present, it is not itself thematized, "thematization"
resulting in its being discursively conceptualized), depicting the pattern of
relationships between Amerigo and Charlotte on the one hand and Maggie
and Adam Verver on the other. Moreover, James extends the metaphor to
depict Maggie's developing awareness of the situation: a dynamic patterned relationship between a particular consciousness and a particular
set of facts with which it must come to terms. The "pagoda" and "chapel/
forge" metaphors are dynamic figurations—epistemic allegories—of the
same order.[10]

The commitment to "show" rather than to "tell about" experience (the
literary artist's rule of thumb) reflects the imaginative writer's predilection
for depiction over explication, perceptual immediacy over discursive
reasoning, synthetic unity over predicative com-positing of analytically
discrete elements. This perceptual bias of the artist is a consequence of the
fact that perception is not in the first instance descriptive, as George
Santayana (no mean literary artist himself) observed: "Perception is . . .
originally true as a signal, but false as a description . . ." (*Obiter Scripta*,
p. 142). Depiction does not refer here to visual imagery; as I argued earlier
in section 1, literary images are not visual (like the print on the page) nor
are they even necessarily picturable (recall, for example, the imagery of
the e. e. cummings poem cited earlier in this chapter). The term is suitable
for the broader connotation intended here, however, because visual perception is perhaps the most rationally accessible and comprehensive field
of immediacy and an ineluctably suggestive model of presentational
awareness, whether such consciousness involves sensuous or nonsensu-
ous (noetic) intuition. Rudolph Arnheim in *Visual Thinking* considers the
visual medium "enormously superior" to what Sir Philip Sidney termed
"wordish descriptions," "because it offers structural equivalents to all

characteristics of objects, events, relations" (p. 232). Visual images commonly present things that are remote both from each other and from the perceiver in varying ways and degrees in a field that is nevertheless uniformly immediate for the perceiver. Similarly, a metaphor like that of the "chapel/forge" in *The Golden Bowl* objectifies experiences and sequences of events of varying remoteness in a presentationally immediate, thematically configured depiction of Adam Verver's character.

As does literary imagery, visual images depict relations that are not actual constitutive elements of the percept, yet of which the percept is more than a mere reflection. Arnheim's comments on "observation by indirection" are pertinent in this connection:

> Distance in depth has no direct equivalent in the two-dimensional projection of the retinal image. The image registers only a gradient of diminishing sizes, and size is one of the factors determining depth perception. Such observation by indirection is . . . also used more consciously in order to measure the inaccessible through some correlated variable, for example, in physics, when temperature is measured by the length of a mercury column. (*Visual Thinking*, p. 41)

The presentational imagery in literary art functions as a correlated experiential variable of the literary theme, conveying conceptual content through the dramatic intensities—the affective power of the ideas—with which it is charged in our awareness.

Consider, for instance, the "cliff / of Norway" metaphor in Allen Tate's "Death of Little Boys" discussed earlier in the context of evaluating interaction theories of metaphor. The theme of the parent's emotional state narratively evolves through descriptive scenes in the bedroom and at the wake to where it veritably bursts with climactic intensity in the depiction of being "assailed" by delirium on the "cliff / Of Norway." Here the grief-drunk parent gazes upon his perilously reeling world. Depictive imagery is the dramatization, or (in Vico's sense) a fable-in-brief, of literary themes that as the occasion of literary metaphor are articulated variously through exposition (as is notably the case in Robert Pirsig's *Zen and the Art of Motorcycle Maintenance*), description, and more encompassing depictions (in allegories such as Spenser's *Faerie Queene*, for instance). As such, metaphor is the antithesis of the discursive analysis that rather than narratively imaging themes *makes* sense of imagery by thematizing it in a universe of discourse that is not literary; analysis thereby articulates themes in schematic *conceptual* as opposed to dramatic *perceptual* terms.

Metaphor thus attests to the essential intermixture of the sensuous and the "intellectual" (i.e., conceptual) that Ernst Cassirer understood as at bottom the way that language means.[11] The cliff of Norway, delirium, and reeling are sensuous images (in contradistinction to images of sense) that serve the intellectual function in Tate's poem of making explicit and dramatically concentrating (and thereby conveying the human value of) the experience of isolation and psychic vertigo that subtly accrue through a progress of nearly overwhelming grief.

Another powerful illustration of this functioning of metaphoric imagery occurs in the sixth stanza of Emily Dickinson's "The Last Night That She Lived."[12] A profoundly perceptive description of a death watch, the poem stands as a brilliant phenomenological study of the witnessing of a death. The penultimate stanza depicts the dying woman at the moment she expires:

> She mentioned and forgot—
> Then lightly as a Reed
> Bent to the Water, struggled scarce—
> Consented, and was dead—

As I have argued elsewhere,[13] Dickinson's dramatization of death through metaphor in this stanza is among the most precise and poignant instances of depictive imagery in the language. The fabling of the final paroxysm as mentioning and then forgetting what it was that one intended to utter invokes—in addition to the vividly explicit presentational image and even visceral response that are concomitants of its enactive envisagement—the archetypal association of death with forgetting. The metaphor of a bent reed worried by a passing breeze that ultimately frees its upper end from the surface of the water dramatizes the conception of death as release, that is, as the termination of strain or tension (doubtless the crucial release for the witness as well). It is an inevitable liberation, one that involves paradoxically enough "consent" of a Pascalian "thinking reed." Alternatively, the reed can be envisaged as bent over and collapsing into the water. The depiction in this case would dramatize capitulation rather than release. The existentially significant consent, however, is conveyed with poignance in both readings.

The power of literary imagery does not derive solely from the way it describes or depicts patterns of relationships. How imagery functions in communicative contexts—its pragmatics—determines its presentational content and hence its aesthetic efficacy.[14] Clichéd images, as in "He's the milk of human kindness" (what Philip Wheelwright cites as an example of

"epiphor"),[15] generally operate descriptively (and so simply designate
or denote). Examples of descriptive imagery used to illustrate analytic
concepts include those such as "Man is a wolf" and "Sally is a block of
ice," figurative phrases that have become so familiar to the theorist of
metaphor as literally to denote the specific studies of Max Black and John
Searle. The physical and social relationships that such images as "milk,"
"wolf," and "block of ice" may be instrumental in depicting (those implicit
in seeing and tasting milk, for instance, or in predatory behavior) do not
present determinate features of "He," "Man," or "Sally" to the degree that
those images are merely descriptive. The reason is that either no narrative
or poetic—i.e., literary experiential—context is present or, typical of the
cliché, the image simply does not dramatize thematic elements of its
context. Imagery of this sort is a form of labeling; it designates but does not
show anything.[16] When metaphorical imagery is clichéd, deadened, the
context, even if richly literary, fails to render the imagery depictive unless
it energizes the depictive potential of the imagery through irony, pun, or
some other means, such as exploiting etymological derivation (which may
be ironic, of course, or used in a pun). Paul Ricoeur would assert that
semantic impertinence is the decisive factor in such cases. And the cognitive theorist Earl R. MacCormac (following Wheelwright) would attribute what I refer to as the "energizing" of depictive potential to occult
cognitive processes triggered by *semantic anomaly* that results from the
juxtaposition of particular referents.

As conceived here, imagery is *significantly depictive* to the extent that,
like the "family coach," it is thematically integrated in a literary work such
that the relationships it depicts *transcend* what it lexically designates (i.e.,
in exclusion of its literary context). Significant depiction subsumes the
denotative sense of descriptive terms by keying, and thus relativizing, the
patterns of relationships that they depict to the presentationally immediate
literary context that occasions them. (It is important to keep in mind that
the reader's act of reading is itself a constitutive factor of the literary
context since it is the sine qua non of any actual presentational literary
event.)[17]

In *Ways of Worldmaking* Nelson Goodman's distinction between depiction and description lends support to the dichotomy posited in the present
analysis.[18] Although he regards depiction in the more restricted, conventional sense, as synonymous with picturing, he considers it a version of

reality that as "vision" is unlike description in not being "literal, denota-tional, and verbal" (p. 102). My conception of depiction includes all of what Goodman lists as nondescriptive "perceptual and pictorial versions and all figurative and exemplificational means" of worldmaking (p. 102). Unlike depiction, description is essentially propositional. Description designates, names; and as W. M. Urban states in *Language and Reality: The Philosophy of Language and the Principles of Symbolism,* "the very meaning of anything immediately universalizes it in some sense and to some degree" (p. 231).[19] More recently, theorists have stressed that naming alienates from the thing named. Robert Scholes explains it this way:

> Human beings become human through the acquisition of language, and the acquisi-tion alienates humans from all those things language names. The name is a substitute for the thing, it displaces the thing in the very act of naming it, so that language finally stands even between one human being and another. Much of our poetry has been written to undo this situation, to remove the veil of language that covers everything with a false familiarity. . . . (*Textual Power,* p. 112)

Since description is propositional, it is different from depiction in that, as C. I. Lewis points out, "what a proposition signifies [as distinct from a propositional function of intention, which involves a participative process of awareness] is some character or attribute of [an] individual, and *not* a part of it" (*Collected Papers,* p. 436).

Literary imagery such as the depictive figures from *The Golden Bowl* explicated in section 2 can be distinguished as significantly depictive—properly metaphorical—as opposed to imagery that is simply descrip-tive.[20] I use the adverb *significantly* to indicate the thematic context of signification that occasions the image—the context that, by depicting, the image dramatizes. Recall, however, that both descriptive and depictive data of literary experience communicate meaning presentationally; but whereas descriptive imagery is discursively composed (constituting what might be called the "narrative baseline" of a work of literary art), depictive imagery, more than merely a vehicle of discourse, *dramatizes* thematically constitutive relational patterns. Regardless of whether the salient physi-cal, social, or conceptual relationships that a literary metaphor depicts have already been or subsequently become metaphorically presented, they nevertheless must function as a denotative, a descriptive, context of meaning if the metaphoric depiction is to be intelligible. Confused "mixed" metaphors result from unruly contexts that, insofar as they fail to present a purely descriptive frame of meaning, undermine the intelligibility of any possible metaphoric depiction.

Since in the actual communication of meaning no sharp line can be drawn a priori between what is descriptive and images that are depictive (since what for some individuals or on certain readings is denotative, for others or on other readings goes beyond designation as a dramatic figuration of meaning), this distinction might appear specious. To conclude this would be mistaken, however, for it would be to presuppose that a discrimination valid in any given instance, to the degree that it is predicated on a set of coherent conceptual principles, must be made in the same way in every instance. That there is no way to fix unequivocally the relational patterns a literary image depicts which *transcend* what the image denotes lexically is of course no reason to doubt that, relative to context (which includes the occasion of the reader's reading), some literary imagery is significantly depictive and some simply descriptive.

But what does it mean to say that imagery *depicts*? It means that imagery renders perceived relationships, or (less abstractly) thoughts and feelings, in a symbolic, presentationally immediate form, and in doing so makes them directly assimilable in the perceiver's experience by dramatizing them in whatever aesthetic (or synesthetic) mode the presentational imagery takes—visual in graphic art, for instance, auditory in music, noetic in literature (insofar as visual and auditory elements do not contribute to the configuration of the meaning communicated).[21] In description (for example, the "precision of moving feet" in the last line of Tate's "Death of Little Boys"), depicted relationships are in the first instance perceived for their own sake, as things in themselves, and not apprehended as an account of any more inclusive frame of meaning. Description thus serves as the "literal" foil of a significantly depictive imagery.

On the other hand, while literary metaphor obviously has a descriptive dimension, that description serves a *depictive* function, in what I am calling *significant* depiction. The familiar "stiff twin compass" image in Donne's "Valediction: Forbidding Mourning," for example, presentationally conveys on the descriptive plane the relationship of the two feet of the device: presenting them expanded, rotated, and contracted. Metaphorically, Donne's image presents—*significantly* depicts—the leave-taker's sense of his and his beloved's relationship and how his travels affect and are affected by the spiritual bond of their mutual love.

On this pragmatic view of literary metaphor any image or trope is metaphorical to the degree that it is significantly depictive, regardless of whether or not it involves a specific locution, such as in the simile. In the case of simile this approach obviates certain vagaries of definition. Consider the following sentence in the entry on simile in the *Princeton Encyclopedia of Poetry and Poetics:*

> At the level of comparison, substitution, or description it is useful to preserve the formal distinction between "metaphor-form" and "simile-form," and to apply the term "submerged s[imile]" to figures of metaphor-form which are in fact similes with the words "like" or "as" omitted. (P. 767)

By conceiving metaphor in a way that avoids the shortcomings of the all-but-discredited comparison and substitution theories, in a way that does not interpret descriptive imagery as operating on the level of meta- phoric experience, the approach to literary metaphor detailed in the present section exorcises the ghostly figure of the formless "submerged simile."[22] In the case of other tropes such as metonymy—association by contiguity (where, for instance, "horse" implies "cavalry")—and its sub- class synecdoche—in which a part stands for the whole or vice versa (as in the use of "wheels" where "automobile" is intended)—the same principle applies when they occur in a literary context: namely, that insofar as the figure transcends a descriptive function to become significantly depictive (presentationally rendering, that is, the theme[s] that occasion it) it is operating metaphorically.

Consider, for instance, the poignant synecdoche centered on "eyes" in the second line—"Surrender their eyes immeasurably to the night,"—of Allen Tate's "Death of Little Boys." The figure is manifestly synecdochic insofar as "Surrender their eyes" dramatizes not only the closing of eyes (and sight) but the closing out of consciousness and life. The dying is not, however, simply indicated, denoted; "surrendering" eyes significantly depicts (and so functions as metaphor by rendering presentational) the thematic content of the opening line—"When little boys grow patient at last, weary"—content that is integrated with, and powerfully amplified by, the trope, which it can be said to occasion. (I ignore for present purposes the proximal metaphors *surrender* and *night* in which "eyes" is embedded and to which it thematically contributes.) The concept of dying that the image centered on "eyes" depicts is that of little boys who, typically possessed of irrepressible vitality, are grown unwontedly "patient at last." Given the poem's title, "last" clearly resonates with the sense of ultimate finality. And the predicate adjective "weary," beyond the normal fatigue that seems so suddenly to overtake energetic children before sleep, images the ineffably distressing *tedium vitae* of the mortally ill little boy.

As a means of elaborating still further the view of literary metaphor being argued for here, it will be useful to probe the concepts of literary imagery and description in the context of Marcus B. Hester's *Meaning of Poetic Metaphor*. Although Hester's analysis diverges in fundamental ways from the present inquiry, it does share the same phenomenological orientation. After considering the literary image and description in light of Hester's study, we will turn to a phenomenological analysis of metaphor by George E. Yoos, which in essential respects anticipates the thrust of the present work.

4. *Two Experiential Approaches to Literary Metaphor*

Marcus B. Hester's *Meaning of Poetic Metaphor: An Analysis in the Light of Wittgenstein's Claim That Meaning Is Use*[23] is a philosophical study that develops a theory of the meaning of poetic metaphor through a "dialogue between authorities on meaning (Wittgenstein and others) and authorities on poetic metaphor (literary critics) . . . " (p. 20). Hester contends that the "unique feature of metaphor," the "most essential metaphorical element" is the process of what Wittgenstein called "seeing as."[24] What gets "seen," the metaphorical image, is a function of "poetic language," language that "presents a fusion of signs and experience" (p. 69). Hester's understanding of poetic language is in line with the conception of literary experience as a presentationally immediate phenomenon: "Poetic language does not so much refer *to* an experience as it presents us with an experience" (p. 68). This statement misleadingly suggests, however, that language communicates experience exclusive of the reader's active, creative engagement. In fact, it stands opposed to Hester's own position on the seminal role of "seeing as" in literary metaphor, which he describes as an "intuitive experience-act."

Hester maintains that the experiential content that poetic metaphor presents is the result of its iconicity, which he defines as the "similarity to a perceptual image" (p. 8). As he explains:

> language in the poem functions iconically through its sense and sound. The most significant way in which metaphor fits this general conclusion is through its two essential aspects, imagery and seeing as. (P. 69)

A poetic image operates iconically when it is metaphorically "seen as," according to Hester, because of "certain sensuous qualities" that the image shares "with its object," qualities that the experience-act of "seeing as" *selects* (p. 150). Hester's account is open to question on this point, however; since "seeing as" in his view is "irreducible" (p. 138) (an epistemological primitive), it can hardly be invoked to explain the principle of selection that determines just what the "relevant aspects of metaphorical imagery" are in any particular instance of poetic metaphor. And given that such selection must vary to suit different images and poetic contexts, the value of the notion of "seeing as" for elucidating how literary metaphor functions is at best dubious.[25]

Hester's observations that "an icon shows while words or signs state" (p. 76) and that "Sentences refer and describe while icons show, represent, and arrange" (p. 76) attest to the depictive and presentational aspects of iconicity that he astutely perceives as functionally identical with the imagery of literary metaphor. Hester's theory of the metaphorical image, on the other hand, is less than satisfactory. In applying the idea of "seeing as"—the "*irreducible* experience-act"—to I. A. Richards's interaction view of metaphor (see the analysis and critique of Richards's theory in chapter 1, section 2), Hester argues that "It is quite important to emphasize that the relation between metaphorical tenor and vehicle is one of 'seeing as' not one of 'recognition' " (p. 172). Two pages further on, he asserts that the vehicle is not " 'recognized' as the tenor, but always 'seen as' the tenor." If the vehicle is *always* "seen as" the tenor, the implication is that the metaphorical image that results from the "seeing as" interaction is contextually determined. The importance of context in the constitution of literary metaphor is something with which few theorists of metaphor would take issue. Hester goes on to state, however, that "Either the tenor or the vehicle in a metaphor may be 'image poor' " (p. 176). If this is so, the question arises as to what there is to be "seen as" if the vehicle constitutes no intelligible image. Conversely, if the tenor is "image poor," how is the vehicle to be "seen as" anything at all?[26]

Hester's difficulty in convincingly articulating the nature of the metaphorical image is nowhere more apparent than when he asserts that "through the metaphor . . . an abstract tenor can be iconicized" (p. 176). If metaphor occurs through the interaction of a vehicle and a tenor (something Hester presupposes by appealing to Richards's theory in the first place), in what way is the abstract meaning of the tenor to be understood as rendered "similar to a perceptual image," that is, iconicized, *through the metaphor*? The vehicle as a perceptual image is not isolable from the dynamic interactive tenor/vehicle complex that composes metaphor on Richards's account. Consequently, to state that the tenor is iconicized through the metaphor explains neither how tenor is iconicized nor, insofar as tenor is thought of as a constitutive element of metaphor, how metaphor functions. Even if we discount Hester's remark on this one point, his entire approach to poetic metaphor is vulnerable to the same telling animadversions that critics have leveled at Richards's theory. Although he does not classify his view as a semantic interaction theory, Hester's foundational notion of irreducible "seeing as" (to the degree that he intends it to imply something more than literally picturable images) is open to the objection that Max Black brought against Richards's use of the terms *interaction, interillumination,* and *cooperation*. Relying on such terms to explain how metaphor works, observes Black, is uncritically "to *use* a metaphor emphasizing the dynamic aspects of a good reader's response to a non-trivial metaphor" (*Models and Metaphors,* p. 39). Finally, Hester's iconic signification theory can have little to recommend it after such searching criticisms as those that John Searle and Israel Scheffler directed against Paul Henle's iconic signification approach (see section 3 of chapter 1). In sum, Hester's position—derived, as he acknowledges, from the views of Langer, Ogden and Richards, and Wheelwright—that metaphorical imagery is presentational rather than abstract is true to the phenomenological dimension of literary experience (the *only* dimension, as I have argued, of *literary* experience). On the other hand, his approach to metaphorical imagery and his conception of the way poetic metaphor functions are less than convincing on a number of counts.

Although problematic, Hester's analysis of metaphor is of interest even beyond his observations about the primacy of the presentational quality of metaphorical imagery. His assertions about description in metaphor bear, if negatively, on the distinction made in the preceding section of the present chapter between descriptive and depictive imagery. By stating that "Sentences refer and describe while icons show, represent and arrange," Hester suggests the description-depiction dichotomy. Yet the basis of Hester's distinction (the difference between a sentence and an image) is questionable in cases where a verbal icon is a grammatical sentence, as when a lawman shouts, "Freeze!" Hester says that "metaphor [is] understood as seeing as between elements of imagistic description" (p. 133). Description refers here to the nonmetaphorical function of literary images. The process that Hester problematically characterizes as "seeing as" corresponds to what I call the depictive use of otherwise descriptive images, or *significant* depiction. Oddly enough, Hester does not regard literal, descriptive language as imagistic: "metaphor essentially involves imagery while literal writing does not" (p. 133). If this is the case, Hester needs to explain the reference of what he terms *imagistic description,* a kind of description that "between elements" of which "seeing as" operates so as to generate metaphor. Consider Hester's formulation of what is "involved" in metaphor: "Metaphor involves not only . . . iconic description, but *involves the intuitive relation of seeing as between parts of the description*" (p. 169).

Imagistic description is thus to be understood as synonymous with iconic description. The contradiction is manifest: "Sentences refer and describe while icons show, represent and arrange," yet, as Hester has it, icons *also* describe. This vitiation of an otherwise important distinction reveals a vicious circularity at the heart of Hester's theory of how poetic metaphor functions. Hester claims that "The most essential metaphorical element, namely seeing as, functions through the iconicity of the meaning of words" (p. 81). Yet he also contends that in metaphor "an abstract tenor can be iconicized" by the process of "seeing as" between it and the vehicle. Hester thus postulates iconicity as a function of the very process ("seeing as") whose efficacy (in rendering an abstract tenor iconic) he invokes iconicity to explain in the first place! Although he distinguishes seminal aspects of aesthetic apprehension, such as the presentational nature of metaphorical imagery, and he discerns (albeit inconsistently) the key distinction in the phenomenological analysis of metaphor between descriptive and depictive language, Hester nevertheless fails to provide a coherent explanation of metaphorical imagery and on that count falls short of articulating a cogent theory of literary metaphor.

While Hester's approach to poetic metaphor shares a number of essential elements with the depictive view introduced here, George E. Yoos's perspective on metaphor is closer to that of the present study than any other analysis with which I am familiar. In a groundbreaking 1971 essay, "A Phenomenological Look at Metaphor," Yoos turns most of the prevailing metaphor theory on its head. He proposes an approach to metaphor that eschews a priori theoretical constructs, such as preconceived or extrinsically derived notions of comparison, interaction, or iconicity. His aim is to show "phenomenologically how metaphors operate or function in our awareness of them" (*Philosophy and Phenomenological Research* 32 [1971], p. 80). Yoos finds the stumbling block of earlier theories in their

> failure to distinguish between the initial phase of *our awareness, apprehension, or use of metaphor* from *our interpretive inferences to the meaning or intent of metaphor.* (P. 81)

Yoos sees this failure of theorists of metaphor as common in art criticism generally,

> where people fail to distinguish between the act of appreciation and the act of analysis of a work of art. When we use or apprehend metaphors we are actually doing something quite different from interpreting metaphors . . . Always the former experience is the ground for establishing the validity of the latter interpretive or analytic activity. (P. 81)

Yoos's insight is confirmed by the less than satisfactory interpretive inferences—inferences that Bergson would have called "ready-made" (*The Creative Mind*, p. 80)—derived from Aristotelian, interaction, and analytic theories of other sorts (see chapter 1, section 3) when applied hermeneutically to works of literature. As noted in the conclusion of chapter 1, Yoos locates the source of such exegetical difficulties in the uncritical shift "from the question of what a metaphor is like descriptively to the question of what we are doing in the name of interpretation" (p. 83). He points out that in the phenomenology of comprehension the evaluation of meaning—i.e., analysis—is secondary, at a conscious remove, from the apprehension of meaning. Yoos infers from this that analysis as such is not a component of awareness in the apprehension of metaphor. This view agrees with W. M. Urban's observation "that the meaning of the metaphor precedes analysis of the metaphor. The given precedes the analysis of it and cannot be completely or perhaps even adequately explained by the analysis" (quoted in Shibles, p. 37).

Yoos indicates a number of significant theoretical implications of this phenomenological approach when he declares that

> There is no necessary awareness of words as such. There is no initial awareness of *verbal* opposition. There is no *necessary* awareness of analogy, likeness, or comparison when we conceive of one object, quality, or action through the form of another. In this respect, metaphor is as literal as any normal statement of fact, description, or statement of identity.[27]

Yoos's emphasis on the language of experience (an emphasis of Hester's theory as well) does not rule out the significance of analytic categories or frames of mind in our encounters with literary metaphor. To paraphrase the familiar Kantian dictum: Experience without analysis is blind, analysis without experience empty. Yoos acknowledges the indispensability of strictly analytic approaches to metaphor in the context of the deliberative task of interpretation (during which literary experience is, as it were, suspended).[28] But in a critique of specific aspects of Black's interaction theory, he astutely delineates the limits of interpretative acts vis-à-vis the comprehension of metaphor. Yoos explains that the analysis of metaphor involves setting up

> a system of assumptions in order to draw out the meaning or the intention of the given constitution of the metaphor. Nevertheless, the process of setting up a system of what are valid assumptions to establish a system of implication as to meaning or intention is *not* to discuss the character or nature of the phenomenon of metaphor. Even though the nature or character of a metaphor relates to its use, the description of metaphor ought not be confused with its use in the context of communication. (P. 86)

Prior to a concluding discussion of the efficacy and limits of analytic (formal) and phenomenological (descriptive) discourse in the construal of literary metaphor, the significance of Yoos's essay, which seems to me as radical a break with prevailing thinking on the topic as the fifth lecture of I. A. Richards's *Philosophy of Rhetoric* was half a century ago, calls for summary in light of the seminal theses of the present work.

1. By drawing a sharp distinction between analytic approaches to metaphor and the phenomenological orientation, Yoos makes clear the theoretical ramifications of the epistemology informing the depictive view of metaphor as they contrast with those of the theories considered in chapter 1.

2. By calling attention to the failure of previous analyses to distinguish between the experiential and pragmatic dimensions of metaphor on the one hand and interpretive inferences as to metaphoric meaning on the other, Yoos paves the way for an approach such as the present one that conceives the experiential and pragmatic aspects of metaphor in the phenomenological terms of presentational immediacy and depiction. This approach takes presentational immediacy and depiction to be phenomena of a universe of discourse that is at a conscious remove from that of analytic interpretive strategies (that nevertheless are instrumental in enhancing presentational awareness and, by extension, literary experience). The two orders of

discourse may be linked "practically" in a pedagogy of literary experience that involves an interanimating dialectic between the phenomenological apprehension of metaphor and a mutually qualifying interplay of phenomenological and formal interpretive inferences as to metaphoric meaning. Literary experience, as I have argued, is a function of *reading* and not the deliberative construal of *a* reading. As the actual aesthetic of the appreciation of literary art, literary experience transcends all approaches to reading, whether analytical (formal) or phenomenological (descriptive). At the close of the upcoming section, explicative phenomenological discourse is employed in the interpretation of a poem by Emily Dickinson to mediate between the discursive, deliberative thinking operative in formal analysis (and which locates all preconditions of intelligibility at a remove from the qualitative character of experience) and the pre-discursive, presentational immediacy of the reading reader's awareness. This is a practical strategy that I employ to foreground the depictive function of metaphor in literary experience.

3. Yoos's discernment of the uncritical shift in most theories of metaphor from descriptive, or phenomenological, explanations to interpretive acts indicates the need for a study such as the present, which not only highlights the problematic of facile shifts between experience and discursive interpretation but endeavors to interpret the fundamental interrelationship between them in the context of the pragmatics of literary metaphor. To the degree that it succeeds, this effort interconnects theory and practice in an area sorely in need of intelligible and practicable integrations.

4. The point that Yoos makes about metaphorical language being "literal"[29] underscores that the depictive use of literary imagery—i.e., its significant depiction—does not preclude its descriptive (denotative) or literal sense. It merely relativizes it to the context that occasions the figure; in other words, it narrativizes description, transforming it, as Vico long ago discerned metaphor to do, into a fable in brief.

5. Yoos's focus on the significance of "use" in the function of metaphor bears out the point, emphasized earlier in section 3, that how imagery is employed determines its presentational content.

6. Finally, by distinguishing the (analytically deduced) nature of metaphor from its "pragmatics" in the "context of communication," Yoos reveals the contextualism that is at the heart of the phenomenological approach to metaphor.

Yoos's "Phenomenological Look at Metaphor" makes it clear that a satisfactory theory of literary metaphor needs to account for the intuitive, prediscursive dimension of awareness characteristic of the fluent apprehension of language.[30] For the "unity of the units of experience," as Stanley Rosen points out, "cannot be explained analytically or constructively" (*Limits of Analysis*, pp. 118–19). And as Yoos observes with respect to literary experience, "Rarely are we attending to words [i.e., analytically isolable components of meaning] in reading" ("A Phenomenological Look," p. 42). As noted in the opening section of chapter 2, however, this does not gainsay the instrumentality of analytic constructs or interpretive strategies in the comprehension and appreciation of literary metaphor. Indeed, any coherent phenomenological theory of literary metaphor must tacitly assume that the deliverances of literary experience are in some measure and for clearly defined purposes translatable into principles of rational inquiry. (It is in this way that at the interface of discursive and prediscursive consciousness metaphor gets implemented as a heuristic device serving speculative ends in the sciences, for instance, where the distinction between the notion of metaphor and those of model, paradigm, and schema is vague at best.)

The value of a cogent, contextually germane interpretive strategy (and context, recall, is understood here to include the situation in which meaning is actualized: i.e., the reader reading) in the comprehension of literary metaphor is manifest when, for example, a reader gets stumped by a difficult, obscure, or otherwise problematic metaphor. At such impasses the conscious state, the spell, of *reading* is broken and the reader commences deliberatively to process, to construe, *a* reading through the mediation of an analysis of metaphoric function, or of rules of interpretation either tacitly or overtly based on such an analysis. This analysis may be *formal*, as when metaphor is understood (à la Black) as a composite of a frame and focus and its explication perceived as the constructing of a secondary (or, in Richards's terminology, a "focal") "implicative complex" that is parallel and that somehow fits the implicative complex of the primary subject (or frame) in terms of which the metaphor operates.

Alternatively, the analysis of a metaphor may be *descriptive*, involving examination of the phenomenology of the reader's literary experience for its own sake (i.e., as it is given), and with a view toward deciphering what the literary image in question depicts. In *Textual Power* Robert Scholes takes a position on the motive for discursive interpretation that is similar to that argued for here, advocating a pedagogy of the literary text based on the triad of reading, interpretation, and criticism.[31] In Scholes's view deliberative interpretation

> depends upon the failures of reading. It is the feeling of incompleteness on the reader's part that activates the interpretive process. This incompleteness can be based upon such simple items as a word the reader cannot understand, or such subtleties as the reader's sense that a text has a concealed or non-obvious level of meaning that can only be found by an active, conscious process of interpretation. (P. 22)

The need for suitable and discerning analytic modes of discourse for understanding and for teaching literary metaphor is not in question. The contention here is that the *initial appeal* and the *final satisfaction* of depictive imagery occur in the context of communication: in literary experience. Insofar as this is actually the case, it follows that explications of literature appropriately begin and find their terminus in the phenomenology of literary experience.[32] However, although depictive imagery can be studied phenomenologically, descriptive or phenomenological analysis *as analysis* does not share the frame of awareness in which the phenomena it explores occur and are self-sufficing embodiments of meaning. As with formal analysis, descriptive analysis *affirms* things of the literary experiential phenomena it scrutinizes; whereas in reading, literary phenomena do not as such affirm, do not stand as truth-functional assertions (although they may be truth-functional incidentally and from a nonliterary perspective), and thus operate on a different plane of meaning.

If the purpose of exegesis is to enhance literary experience, once an explication is completed—once it has pointed the way for the act of reading—analysis whether formal or descriptive (or some combination) must fall silent before—permit, in the etymological sense of "letting go in the face of" or "surrendering to"—renewed acts of reading. Given the limits of analysis, the discourse that is employed to explicate literary metaphor, even if it is phenomenological, at its best no more than adumbrates literary experience.

5. *Understanding Literary Metaphor*

This closing section is largely concerned with what it means to explicate literary experience and, more specifically, literary metaphor from the perspective of two diverse universes of discourse: that of abstract reflection and conceptualization and that of the phenomenological idiom of presentational experience. The section, and with it this study of the depictive image, concludes with a brief explication of a metaphor centered in the final stanza of Emily Dickinson's "A Bird Came Down the Walk," the same poem that I considered in the critique of Aristotelian theories of metaphor in the opening chapter. Along with the discussion in section 2 of extended metaphors in *The Golden Bowl*, the analysis of the metaphor in Dickinson's poem illustrates how the approach to metaphor and literary experience articulated here and in the preceding chapter enhances, rather than merely pays lip service to or mystifies, practical criticism. Before taking up the interpretive implications of formal and descriptive ways of apprehending metaphor, a brief summary of the cardinal points pertaining to the notion of literary metaphor as a depictive image will set in relief the conceptual frame of the discussion.

The depiction of the depictive image is the prereflective, presentational rendering of patterned relationships (physical, social, psychological, etc.) among entities and events that, to the degree that they get descriptively presented, serve as the context of signification of the image. The significant mode of depiction, as distinguished from what might be called the "designational presentation" of purely descriptive imagery, is what literary metaphor effects. The presentational character of literary experience in general is a function of reading, which attests to the communicative, indeed communal, medium of literary metaphor. In assuming a presentational form, imagistically depicted relational patterns dramatize the thematic meaning that those patterns express and amplify in their literary context.

All this occurs in what Ernst Cassirer would call the "mythic" apprehension of the audience of a work of literary art as it attends to what, from a discursive, analytic perspective, are phenomenological correlatives of universal schemes of meaning constitutive of the work's intelligibility. Within the context of literary experience, however, there is no "correlation" between meaning in the abstract (for example, the idea in *The Golden Bowl* of Adam Verver's having turned intense cerebral energy profitably to account in the world of business) and the data of presentational awareness (such as the vivid forge image that operates as a pocket drama—in Vico's sense, a fable in brief—in James's characterization of the wealthy American art collector). This is so because in mythic thinking the two are inextricably commingled, in fact indistinguishable, in the prediscursive (phenomenological) apprehension of meaning. The distinction presupposed for such a correlation derives from, and is intelligible only within, the universe of discourse within which deliberative, formal analysis operates.

This is not to deny or undervalue the significance of the experiential index that attests to the interanimation of ideas and phenomenological data in depictive imagery. This index of the efficacy of ideas rendered presentationally, and by extension the interanimation of ideas and percepts, is the experience of *drama* generated by literary art; for in drama judgment and perception are combined on a prediscursive plane of awareness. This is in marked contrast with conceptual analysis, where perception is held in suspension, as it were, and judgment, not simply a concomitant of *presence*, follows from inferences derived from anatomizing the object. Put another way, analytical judgment operates at a conscious remove from how things impact phenomenologically in the field of presentational awareness that is exclusive of the mitigating factor of interpretive effort. In literary experience, where abstract ideas are cast as *happenings*, patterned relationships get dramatized either as descriptions or as depictions; they are thereby objectified as perceptual data rather than abstractly schematized as bloodless categorical terms of signification.

The concept of the image presupposed in the notion of the depictive image is not intended to suggest a reified idea, since that would imply a difference between an idea proper and particular objective manifestations of it, something that is inconceivable in the world of literary experience (where form and meaning are never disjunct). As understood here, the literary image is a field phenomenon and not any sort of determinate ideal construct. It is a disposition of consciousness (not marks on a page nor some ineffable "content" of a mind) that the intelligible data of phenomenological experience assume as the very condition of their being intelligible. Images commonly operate denotatively, as labels in discursive and dialectical thinking, where they serve as descriptive vehicles in the development of thought. Beyond a strictly descriptive function, however, images also operate as dramatic, narrative phenomena that articulate thought depictively and in so doing constitute its very idiom.

Regardless of whether they work denotatively as descriptive vehicles in the development of literary themes or whether they serve as the depictive medium of thematic amplification, literary images convey patterned relationships among entities and events presentationally. It is in this mode of aesthetic, presentational awareness that literary themes are perceptible as such and in their uniqueness, rather than as exemplifications of abstract schemas, be they mythic, psychological, linguistic, semiotic, or whatever.

And it is in the presentational immediacy of literary experience that literary images articulate and amplify thematic meaning. This realization of meaning occurs in the communicative context of a reader reading (the actual occasion of awareness in which we perceive themes as phenomena) and in the progression of conscious apprehension in terms of which themes can be said literally to develop. As the experiential, the only actual, medium of thematic development, the communicative context of literary experience is the epistemological context of literary metaphor. The meaning of (literary) metaphorical meaning is thus rooted in the literary experience of the reader. A "presenting" of thematic meaning, literary metaphor is a seminal dynamic in the transformation of the *wherefore* of conscious apprehension into the very condition *of* consciousness. Put another way, metaphor is the principal epistemic means by which we transform the experience of what we do—which in literary reading involves going beyond ourselves—into that of what we are.

This transformative power of metaphor in literature is an expression of the creative, the self-transcending (or ecstatic) dimension of literary reading. The experiencing of literary art is as such ecstatic, mimetic in the performative pre-Platonic sense. Literary reading is thus a "moving outside" of our wonted frame of awareness to participate in the process of vision that the writer makes available through what Monroe Beardsley described as the "arrangement of conditions [i.e., the composing of a text] intended to be capable of affording an experience with marked aesthetic presentational character" (quoted by Dempster, p. 153). By his complementary participation in the literary enterprise, the reader celebrates artistic vision in the only way that the communicative endeavor of the artist is ever actively celebrated.

The degree to which a literary metaphor's thematic meaning takes place prereflectively, depictively (in what we might call its operational context) determines the extent to which its transformative power is realized. And just as virtually no bounds exist to the possible refinement of human experience and sensibility, so there are none to limit metaphor's power to transform us by being our means of assimilating novel and ever more richly discriminated data of awareness. By the same token, reading a literary metaphor is inert and fails to amplify experience to the extent that the reader is not in tune with its depictive power in context, and is thus out of touch with the themes that it stands to articulate and convey presentationally.

As noted at the conclusion of chapter 1, the most influential theories of metaphor typically evolve from insights into metaphoric efficacy—what metaphor does—and account insufficiently for how metaphor operates. To explain *what* metaphor does in terms of *how* calls for an explanation of the experiential situation in which metaphor actually functions and that serves as the medium in which it is apprehended as such in the first place. This is something that rationalist theorists (at bottom, conceptual idealists) since Aristotle have in great measure neglected as a result of the subject-object bias of their approach. The consequence in metaphor scholarship has been a profusion of theories on the nature of metaphoric experience with few, if any, criteria for selecting among alternative approaches in practical criticism. There has been little in the way of net gain in practical understanding of how literary metaphor operates, and this is because there have been few inquiries into how metaphoric experience in *literature* is a function of *literary* experience.

Max Black summarized the problem of metaphor for rationalist theorists when in 1978 he found himself still puzzling, as I noted earlier, over what it means to say that in metaphor "one thing is thought of (or viewed) *as* another thing" (in Sacks, p. 192). The preposition that Black emphasizes indicates the explanatory limit of approaches to metaphor that are essentially acontextual and analytic. To conceive something *as* something else—assuming that metaphor actually involves a coupling of some sort—is a *synthetic* act. Formal analysis can account for synthesis, but only in a domain of discourse in which the limit of intelligibility is founded on the assumption that for any given situation either *A* or *not-A* is the case—period; and that while different things may be said to share properties, there is just no telling how they lend them to one another.

Setting the stage for a consideration of literary metaphor that transcends the limits of formal analysis, the discussion of literary experience in chapter 2 detailed the phenomenological context in which literary metaphor comes to be and provided an epistemological rationale for conceiving metaphor as a depictive image. The underlying assumption is that any understanding of what a particular literary metaphor does must be geared to how metaphor functions in literary experience generally. A principal aim of the present chapter, and in particular section 3, has been to explain metaphoric functioning in the context of literary experience.

I turn next to practical considerations related to the construal of literary metaphor. Both formal (rationalistic, schematic) and descriptive (phenomenological, experiential) modes of analytic discourse play an indis-

pensable role in conveying and enhancing understanding of literary metaphor; hence both are essential to the enrichment of literary experience.
Before illustrating this in the explication with which this study concludes,
it will pay to digress a bit to discuss the interrelation, indeed the interdependence, of formal and descriptive analysis in practical criticism.

In his accessible yet uncompromisingly rigorous *Limits of Analysis*,
Stanley Rosen examines the nature and bounds of formal analysis vis-à-vis
phenomenological experience. *Limits of Analysis* is concisely argued and
rich with insights into what formal analysis is and how it relates to, and in
fact presupposes, prediscursive awareness. And it provides a sound philosophical rationale for the hermeneutic of literary metaphor adumbrated in
the present study.

Rosen points out that "Analytical thinking, rigorously and consistently
understood, requires simple elements" (p. 109). Simple elements out of
which critical theorists construct approaches to literature include everything from the morpheme to the mythic or psychological archetype to the
primitive "asemantic 'drift' " between signifier and signified dubbed by
Jacques Derrida "différance."[33] The problem is to reconcile the analytically predetermined conditions or components of meaning with the synthetic whole of meaning that they are invoked to explain, or explain away.

In the domain of semantics, for instance, Benjamin Hrushovski identifies what he terms the "First-Sentence Fallacy," which as he explains in
"An Outline of Integrational Semantics" is "the analysis of a sentence as if
it stood alone." Hrushovski takes to task semantic theorists who presume
that the basic component of meaningful language is the sentence. "There
are no first sentences in language," argues Hrushovski:

> The "first sentences" of children are highly embedded in their (non-verbal) con-
> text. . . . We must abandon the notion that sentences are the units of mean-
> ing. . . . there is a fallacy assuming that semantics lies in discrete, static units,
> rather than (possible or potential) constructs, sometimes based on diffuse bodies of
> text. (*Poetics Today* 3 [1982]: 61–62)

Implicitly suggesting the need for a semantic of literary experience,
Hrushovski notes that "Interpretations of literary texts involve primarily
understanding of language. A theory of language must be able to account
for the modes in which meanings are conveyed in literary texts" (p. 62).

Over half a century before the publication of Hrushovski's essay, Ernst
Cassirer introduced a holistic, phenomenological view of language (one to
which the approach to the literary image in the present inquiry is sig-

nificantly indebted) to account for meaning without appealing to simple elements—in this case, on the level of the word—as the fundamental units that in some form of aggregate constitute language. Cassirer pointed out that

> As far back as we can trace it, language confronts us as a whole. None of its utterances can be understood as a mere juxtaposition of separate words; in each and every one we find provisions which serve to express the *relation* between the particular elements, and which articulate and graduate their relation in a variety of ways. (*Philosophy of Symbolic Forms*, vol. 1, p. 304)

The relation of the whole to the part is perhaps the most insistent dilemma that analysis of any sort faces in the interpretative engagement with the literary text, and more particularly with literary metaphor. In the context of practical criticism, its most famous formulation is the *hermeneutic circle*. From the perspective of the approach to literary experience undertaken in this study, the hermeneutic circle is no more than a fallacy of equivocation. As Richard Rorty describes it, the hermeneutic circle is the situation

> that we cannot understand the parts of a strange culture, practice, theory, language, or whatever, unless we know something about how the whole thing works, whereas we cannot get a grasp on how the whole works until we have some understanding of its parts. (*Philosophy and the Mirror of Nature*, p. 319)

The whole in the case of literary metaphor is a field of meaning that I have called a depictive image, and which is not susceptible of being understood as it functions in literary experience if taken as a mere aggregation of parts (an "all") related to each other through some occult process of, say, comparison, transfer, or interaction. One of the most trenchant criticisms of the theories of metaphor reviewed in chapter 1 is that they provide no coherent explanation of "how the whole works" that constitutes a rationale for their particular discrimination of the elements of metaphor. In fact, the whole of metaphor that such analytically grounded views claim to explain is frequently a straw man, as Hrushovski has discerned (see chapter 1, note 50). And it should be clear that every rationalist approach to literary metaphor explains the whole in terms of its parts, while the elements selected as parts derive from ways of processing information (such as theories of rhetoric, linguistics, semiotics, deconstruction, and psychoanalysis) that may generate perspectives on literary experience but that cannot account for it nonreductively as it actually occurs (i.e., in its own aesthetic terms).

This suggests the fallacy that, in view of the phenomenological perspective which I have detailed, attaches to the hermeneutic circle. The notion of *understanding* in Rorty's definition has two different senses. The understanding of "parts" as such, parts that taken collectively constitute an additive collocation, or an "all," is not the same as the understanding of "wholes" as such, a concept that is unintelligible without a complementary notion of *components*, which in some sense intrinsically interconnect. The first sort of understanding is a function of formal, discursive thinking that constitutes a universe of discourse where the criteria of coherence—the preconditions of intelligibility—are tied to predicative meaning (where *A* has meaning only if there is some *B* that can be predicated of it.)[34] Put another way, a minimum condition of the intelligibility of an entity in formal reasoning is that we be able to distinguish what "belongs" to it. As Stanley Rosen cautions, however, "To say that p belongs to S is not to explain what 'belonging' means" (*Limits of Analysis*, p. 113).[35]

Rosen states a corollary of this inability to account for the connectedness of parts that is at the heart of predicative understanding when he affirms that "We cannot arrive at the unity of a whole by listing the set of predicates, even upon the very rash assumption that the list is complete" (p. 107).[36] Thus by generating understanding through determining and arranging components that it predicates of the literary image, the analysis of literary metaphor cannot in principle provide anything like a holistic understanding of its object. Rosen in fact regards "unity *qua wholeness*" as transcending formal analysis altogether and belonging to "a universal dimension in which formal characteristics are embedded in an unformalizable process" (p. 127). In the context of the present discussion, that process is simply literary experience.

The understanding of wholes as such (and not merely as aggregates or com-positions of parts) occurs on the plane of prereflective, phenomenological awareness in which the meaningful is a matter of *presence* rather than of *predication*. (And it is consistent with this that I term the holistic, thematically configured manifestation of literary meaning for the reader in the act of reading the "presentational immediacy of literary experience.") Although discursive and prediscursive types of understanding are not mutually exclusive, indeed presuppose each other in communicable experience of any sort, they are clearly alternative modalities of awareness. The familiar problem of the whole being more than the sum of its parts is thus a clue that the hermeneutic circle is not a circle at all but rather the reification of the process of analytic dialectic, which assimilates (and thereby reduces) phenomenological data to the categories of formal understanding.

This focusing on the limits of analysis is not to suggest that ascertaining predicates of a depictive image is a waste of effort in our attempts to acquire or convey metaphoric insight.[37] It merely underscores the fact that discursive analysis always implicates a prediscursive domain of meaning (whether openly acknowledged, part of some hidden agenda, or uncritically presupposed) that makes it feasible and significant,[38] a domain of meaning that consequently must be taken into account in the evaluation of what an analysis of literary metaphor actually accomplishes. In the sciences, this factoring-in is virtually built in to the empirical method and so occurs more or less as a matter of course. In the humanities, however, especially in aesthetics, the context of analysis does not systematically or even verifiably relate to a universally sanctioned method or approach to experience. As a consequence, it is frequently lost sight of or remains unaccounted for. This state of affairs is manifest in the failure George E. Yoos discerns in art criticism that neglects to "distinguish between the act of appreciation and the act of analysis of a work of art" ("A Phenomenological Look at Metaphor," p. 165). Clifford Geertz sees this as a problem of Western formalist aesthetics generally, one that undermines the comparative study of the arts:

> The approach to art from the side of Western aesthetics (which as Kristeller has reminded us, only emerged in the mid-eighteenth century, along with our rather peculiar notion of the 'fine arts'), and indeed from any sort of prior formalism, blinds us to the very existence of the data upon which a comparative understanding of it could be built. And we are left, as we used to be in studies of totemism, caste, or bride-wealth—and still are in structuralist ones—with an externalized conception of the phenomenon supposedly under intense inspection but actually not even in our line of sight. (*Local Knowledge*, p. 98)

Without a mediating link between formal analysis and its object (such as that provided by keying the experiential context of analysis to that of the apprehension of the work of art), the rational function of analysis—to make sense of (not to impose sense arbitrarily upon) human experience—is vitiated. To pursue a formal analysis without taking into consideration a mediating ground in light of which to gauge the pertinence of interpretation with respect to its object is to engage in *absolute* analysis. Analytic positivism of this sort tacitly fits experience to a priori formal categories that underlie and serve as the conditions of coherence for a given order of reasoning. It thereby restricts the possible meaning of any literary experience to a set of assumptions that are extrinsic to that experience.

In chapter 2 I discussed literary experience as the mediating factor be-

tween analysis, whether formal or descriptive, and the enactive envisagement of literary metaphor. The alternative to absolute analysis is analytic
relativism, which need not be anarchic. Exclusive of a concrete hermeneutic situation (involving a particular reader at a specific time and place
endeavoring to interpret a given literary metaphor), no one analytic approach is inherently superior to any other—for which reason I subscribe
to an analytic pluralism. In doing so I regard interpretive claims about
literary metaphor that exceed the warrant of their literary-experiential
context as of heuristic (methodological) value rather than of explicitly
exegetical value. Assertions, for instance, that literary metaphor is a comparison, condensation, or an interaction of meaning exceed the warrant of
literary experience in that phenomenological deliverances of depictive
images do not present such processes (which analyses impute to them),
unless of course they constitute literary themes that as topics of literary
imagery get depicted.

The foregoing observations on analysis, literary experience, and metaphor
delineate the theoretical assumptions that inform the explication with
which this study concludes. The analysis of the metaphor centered in the
final stanza of Emily Dickinson's "A Bird Came Down the Walk" coordinates formal (predicative) and experiential (descriptive, textually idio-
matic) discourse and illustrates how the metaphor depicts themes in the
poem that occasion it[39]—that is, how it functions in the context of literary
experience. The themes that occasion a literary metaphor, and which
in rendering presentational the metaphor depicts, can be formulated as
propositions that in a general way "define" the metaphor. How such propositions are initially derived in any given case is a matter of analytic orientation and (in view of the analytic pluralism of the present study) not an
issue here. However, the phenomenological organization and expression
that a depictive image effects of such propositions require meticulous
scrutiny if we are to determine how a literary metaphor functions in its
thematic matrix. Since the analysis of a literary metaphor most readily
begins at the center of the depictive image and radiates outward, that is the
strategy I will adopt in what follows.
    Given the unlimited variability of hermeneutic situations (different
readers reading at different times, interpreting meaning with different presuppositions and ends in view), no hard-and-fast rule can be formulated on
how to educe fruitful propositions that both define and help to elucidate
particular metaphors. The propositions that one selects, however, should
characterize the metaphoric center (*swim* in the instance of the Dickinson

poem) and should express ideas that constitute significant aspects of the
metaphor's thematic occasion. In practical terms, formulating such propositions is a trial-and-error process that, like any intelligent and iterative
effort at interpreting and communicating aesthetic experience, grows less
random and more attuned to nuance with practice. Of course, some propositions that define a metaphoric image more accurately and comprehen-
sively spell out the themes in terms of which the image functions than
others. An explication could approach the ideal limit of accuracy and
comprehensiveness, and thereby reveal the complete integration of a
metaphor with its context, only by determining a set of propositions that
completely exhausts the possible ways in which, as a field of meaning, the
metaphor depicts the concepts-become-story (literary themes) that occasion it. Further, since in literary experience the reader's consciousness
is the source of the "process" in the metaphoric process, it too must be
included as a factor in calculating the ideal limit of accuracy and comprehensiveness in the propositional analysis of literary metaphor. Given
the possibility, however, of many plausible, although mutually exclusive
readings of any particular metaphor, the ideally complete propositional
analysis of literary metaphor is an untenable goal. Practical criticism can
do no more than strive to meet the particular exigencies of the hermeneutic
situation at hand; for the propositional analysis of literary metaphor this
includes recognizing the provisional nature of any subject-object account
of literary experience.

Keeping in mind then the limits of an analysis that combines formal and
descriptive discourse, consider three propositions that in a general way
define the "swimming" depicted in the last line of the poem below (propositions that imagery and imagistic action throughout the poem exemplify
and, by so doing, amplify the metaphoric depiction of the "swim" image
with which the verse concludes):

> A Bird came down the Walk—
> He did not know I saw—
> He bit an Angleworm in halves
> And ate the fellow, raw,
>
> And then he drank a Dew
> From a convenient Grass—
> And then hopped sidewise to the Wall
> To let a Beetle pass—
>
> He glanced with rapid eyes
> That hurried all around—

They looked like frightened Beads, I thought—
He stirred his Velvet Head

Like one in danger, Cautious,
I offered him a Crumb
And he unrolled his feathers
And rowed him softer home—

Than Oars divide the Ocean
Too silver for a seam—
Or Butterflies, off Banks of Noon
Leap, plashless as they swim.

(*Complete Poems*, p. 156)

The focal idea in "as they swim" is swimming, which the following predicates characterize (others equally germane could have been selected):
(1) is a form of directed movement, (2) is patterned motion, (3) occurs
within a liquid medium. The first predicate is exemplified by the bird's
flight. Flying, however, is not the only type of directed movement the bird
displays: earlier it hops "down the Walk." The flight at the end is escape.
The poem thus opens with a movement of approach, emphasized by the
verb *came*, and closes with one of departure. The concluding stanza amplifies the theme of directed movement by shifting from the image of oars that
indeterminately "divide the Ocean" to that of butterflies in self-directed
"Leap[s], *off* Banks of Noon" (emphasis added). Rather than between
"Oars" and "Butterflies," the parallel, if it were exact, would be between
oars and butterflies' *wings*. Dickinson has larger purposes in mind, however, and, as with her use of off-rhyme, she tailors form to convey the
richest amplitude of insight. In this instance, the subtle shift to "Butterflies" depicts the transition of perceptual concentration from the movement of the bird's wings to that of the bird as a whole and totally immersed
in the ambient air. A net effect of this is that "all" of the bird's movement—a thematic of the poem—is perceived to culminate in *swim*, the
center of the metaphoric image that depictively resolves the theme.

Understood as an idea that develops in the reading of the poem, the second concept that the predicate articulates "emplots"[40] (schematizes the
narrative function of) two thematic trajectories. The first can be traced in
the increasing gracefulness of the motion depicted in the verse: from
biting, eating, and drinking to hopping sidewise, in the first two stanzas;
from rapidly glancing eyes and the stirring of head-feathers in the central
stanza, where the bird remains stationary; to the unfolding of wings and a

motion of rowing to that of silent butterfly strokes in the liquid noontide air in the penultimate and closing quatrains. The second trajectory is the thematic of decreasing pace (a concomitant of the accruing grace), which conveys presentationally the sense of decelerating time, culminating in a fixed scene (emblematic of the poem as a totality). This occurs through the identification of the bird's movement with rowing and partial immersion in a liquid medium; with butterflies in flight; and finally its identification with the motion of swimming (in the form of a splashless leaping that suggests complete immersion), in an image that depicts the slowed motion of flight in an ambient substantially sensuous as liquid.

In the fourth stanza the image of rowing emplots the predicate "occurs in a liquid medium." The "dividing" that in a liquid medium leaves no seam, along with the leaping "off Banks of Noon" that causes no splashing, creates the impression that action, since it has no causal impact on its setting, is no less than *part of the place* in which it occurs. Dickinson in effect suspends with a spatial fixity the bird's flight, renders it "motionless in motion" (to borrow an oxymoron from Archibald MacLeish's "Calypso's Island").

While the metaphoric *swim* of butterflies dramatizes the grace of their flight, it also communicates with presentational immediacy the concepts of *directed movement, patterned motion,* and *an occurrence in a liquid medium,* which serve as elements of the poem's architectonics. As moments of the verse's conceptual framework that get depicted concretely in the imagery, these ideas are themes that, along with a virtually indefinite number of possible alternatives or variations consistent with coherent readings, are interdependent in the poem, most notably in the final two stanzas where each comes to implicate the others. The swim of butterflies—a fable in brief—depictively unifies the three themes and in so doing imagistically amplifies their topic, the bird's flight.

By articulating themes depictively, metaphors lend the ever-fresh intensities of the life-world to the meanings that literary artists communicate. The eighteenth-century aesthetician Alexander Baumgarten observed that "the figures of the poet return to language the immediacy of feeling and sensation,"[41] something, we might add, that analytic discourse abstracts. When a metaphor "dies," becomes purely descriptive, it no longer conveys that sense of life; as Nelson Goodman has noted, in a "frozen" metaphor "What vanishes is not its veracity but its vivacity" (*Languages of Art,* p. 68).

Living experience is what literary metaphor communicates and our perceptual life is what informs the way it communicates. To apprehend a literary metaphor in its narrative or poetic context is an enactment, indeed a celebration, of the vital immediacies and refinements of sensibility and awareness that artists have always turned to metaphor to depict.

NOTES

Introduction

1. Adena Rosmarin, "Theory and Practice: From Ideally Separated to Pragmatically Joined," *Journal of Aesthetics and Art Criticism* 43 (1984):31–40.

2. See Benjamin Hrushovski, "Poetic Metaphor and Frames of Reference," *Poetics Today* 5 (1984):5.

3. Paul Ricoeur, *The Rule of Metaphor*, trans. Robert Czerny with Kathleen McLaughlin and John Costello (Toronto, 1977), pp. 131–32. In the second volume of *Time and Narrative*, trans. Kathleen McLaughlin and David Pellauer (Chicago, 1985), Ricoeur defines discourse "in the strict sense of the word" as "a succession of sentences presenting their own rules of composition" (p. 30).

4. As Wilbur Marshall Urban explains in an extended essay on Ernst Cassirer's philosophy of language,

> Predication, in the logical sense, is but the conceptual expression of relations already intuited. . . . The logical concept . . . does nothing else than fix the "gesetzliche Ordnung" [lawful ordering] already present in the phenomena themselves, it states consciously the rule which the perception follows unconsciously. ("Cassirer's Philosophy of Language," in *The Philosophy of Ernst Cassirer*, ed. Paul Arthur Schilpp [1949; rpt. La Salle, 1973], pp. 415–16)

5. As Susan L. Feagin notes,

> Metaphor can never be identical with its paraphrase any more than art is identical with its interpretation. . . . To understand a metaphor as a metaphor, it is not sufficient to turn it into something else, a literal statement. The language which is used metaphorically is often responsible for the character of the imagining which is performed to understand it, so that a literal paraphrase leaves out exactly what is effective about the metaphor. ("Some Pleasures of Imagination," *Journal of Aesthetics and Art Criticism* 43 [1984]:51–52)

6. See Samuel R. Levin, *The Semantics of Metaphor* (Baltimore, 1977), p. 4.

7. W. V. Quine, *From a Logical Point of View*, 2d ed. (New York, 1961), p. 42. Such "term-by-term empiricism" is the philosophical root of theories that regard the operation of metaphor as an additive process of predication.

8. Mark Johnson, ed. *Philosophical Perspectives on Metaphor* (Minneapolis, 1981).

9. Giambattista Vico's view of metaphor as a way of experiencing facts is the most significant earlier divergence from the Aristotelian perspective. See Terence Hawkes's brief comments on Vico's theory of metaphor, in *Metaphor* (New York, 1972), pp. 38–40. For a comprehensive study of Vico's thinking, see Donald Phillip Verene, *Vico's Science of Imagination* (Ithaca, 1981). Vico was an important influence on Coleridge, whose non-Aristotelian philosophy of the imagination Hawkes discusses in connection with the idea of metaphor (pp. 42–56). (A study of Coleridge's considerable impact on the thinking of I. A. Richards would doubtless reveal the sources of Richards's non-Aristotelian conception of the metaphoric process.)

10. "Mimesis" is intended here in its pre-Platonic sense; see W. Tatarkiewicz, "Mimesis," *Dictionary of the History of Ideas*, ed. Philip P. Weiner (New York, 1973), vol. III, p. 226; see also Mihai Spariosu, *Mimesis in Contemporary Theory* (Philadelphia, 1984), pp. I–III.

1. Metaphor

1. This determination holds both in a positive *and* in a negative sense. See, for instance, Karl Popper's distinction between a theory's "empirical content" and its "informative content" ("the set of statements which are incompatible with the theory") in *Unended Quest* (La Salle, 1976), p. 26.

2. See *The Limits of Analysis* (New York, 1980), p. 222. Rosen classifies *diaeresis* as a *techne*, a process of creating artificial constructs. As such, *diaeresis* "shapes natural beings or 'stamps' them with a constructed form" (p. 222). Probing the characteristics of Platonic analysis, Rosen finds that in explaining things by the method of *diaeresis*, the "empirical object is replaced in the process of analysis by the scientific, mathematical or eidetic structure" (p. 108). The consequence in the theory of metaphor of this "replacement" or refashioning of the immediate deliverances (the aesthetics) of experience is a key concern, indeed the raison d'être, of the present study.

3. Commenting on the influence of Aristotle's discussions of metaphor, Mark Johnson concludes that

> After Aristotle there followed over twenty-three hundred years of elaboration on his remarks. From a philosophical point of view, at least, virtually every major treatment up to the twentieth century is prefigured in Aristotle's account. (*Philosophical Perspectives on Metaphor* [Minneapolis, 1981], p. 8)

Notable among others who have made the same point is Umberto Eco. Though overstating the case somewhat, Eco finds that

> of the thousands and thousands of pages written about metaphor, few add anything of substance to the first two or three fundamental concepts stated by Aristotle. ("The Scandal of Metaphor: Metaphorology and Semiotics," *Poetics Today* 4 [1983]:217–18)

4. *The Works of Aristotle*, ed. W. D. Ross (Oxford, 1924), vol. XI. The familiar clause, "a good metaphor implies an intuitive perception of the similarity in dissimilars," may

appear at first glance to be Aristotle's definition of metaphor as a figure or trope based on similarity. Positing what "a good metaphor implies" about a maker of metaphor is not, however, to explain how a metaphor operates in conscious apprehension.

5. W. B. Stanford, *Greek Metaphor: Studies in Theory and Practice* (Oxford, 1936).

6. Consider, for example, Gumpel's initial explanation of the third of the three "trichotomies of ontic heteronomy" that she introduces as the basis of her approach to metaphor:

> *Argument* accounts for the one adequated "literal" use which operates through the acquisition of a reality-nexus in the juxtaposition between a pure and an objective referent. Conversely, *Dicent* and *Rheme* present two non-adequated counterparts that draw only on the pure referent, for which reason alone they attain their *literary* status as respective fictional and lyric genres. Theirs will be a difference in size of constitutional unit(y), with an extended transference obtaining for the Rheme. . . . The Micro-component of the Rheme subjugated to this modification evolves as a functional non-Aristotelian metaphor. (*Metaphor Reexamined: A Non-Aristotelian Perspective* [Bloomington, 1984], pp. 59–60)

7. "Metaphor," says Aristotle in the *Poetics* (1457b), "consists of giving the thing a name that belongs to something else; the *transference* being from genus to species, or from species to genus, or from species to species, or on grounds of analogy" (emphasis added).

8. In addition to *Poetics* (1457b), see the *Rhetoric* (1406b and 1410b).

9. "Until recently," states Black, "one or another form of a substitution view has been accepted by most writers (usually literary critics or writers of books on rhetoric) who have anything to say about metaphor" (*Models and Metaphors: Studies in Language and Philosophy* [Ithaca, 1962], p. 31). Johnson, for one, takes a different view of the matter: "The comparison theory has been the single most popular and widely held account of how metaphor works" (*Philosophical Perspectives*, p. 25).

10. Donald Davidson compellingly, though controversially, argues against any distinction between the literal and the figurative sense of an expression in metaphorical meaning. See "What Metaphors Mean," in *On Metaphor*, ed. Sheldon Sacks (Chicago, 1979), pp. 29–45. For a suggestive discussion of metaphor that is sympathetic with Davidson's views, see Stephen Davies's "Truth-Values and Metaphors," in *The Journal of Aesthetics and Art Criticism* 42 (1984):291–302.

11. Gumpel claims that this transference occurs

> not as a function based on juggled categories and proxy-barter [in Gumpel's theory, the basis of semantic transfer between denotative and lexically deviant meaning]. Rather, the meanings chosen to engender authorial intent undergo a *shift* as their explicit denomination releases the implicit connotations relevant to the constitutional unit(y) as in [Gumpel's] book's every sentence. (P. 4)

What Gumpel refers to as transfer based on "juggled categories" is an assumption of approaches to metaphor such as Nelson Goodman's (see *Languages of Art* [Indianapolis, 1976], p. 73).

By "proxy-barter," Gumpel means metaphorical substitution, where "(proper) *description* is replaced by the (improper) redescribing agent." In this connection she cites Paul Ricoeur's position that metaphor is a form of redescription resulting from a deliberate deconstructive category-mistake (see *Metaphor Reexamined*, p. 256). Gumpel maintains that her approach relies on the notion of a "structurally based" transference of meaning in metaphor; and that, since her theory does not postulate "violated categories and proxytenet substitutions" (p. 4), it is actually non-Aristotelian. Aristotle never speaks, however, of "violations" of categories or of "category-mistakes" (a concept made prominent in critical discourse by Gilbert Ryle in *The Concept of Mind* [New York, 1949]). Ricoeur makes this same point early in his *Rule of Metaphor* (Toronto, 1977), p. 21.

12. Rom Harré, in *The Philosophies of Science* (New York, 1972), refers to analogy as a "relationship" that "allows inferences" between the two terms:

> An analogy is a relationship between two entities, processes, or what you will, which allows inferences to be made about one of the things, usually that about which we know least, on the basis of what we know about the other. . . . The art of using analogy is to balance up what we know of the likenesses against the unlikenesses between two things, and then on the basis of this balance make an inference as to what is called the neutral analogy, that about which we do not know. (P. 172)

Although he avoids explicit allusion to comparison, Harré clearly presupposes the notion in his definition. Note that substitution plays no role in analogy in Harré's account.

13. Warren Shibles, *An Analysis of Metaphor in the Light of W . M . Urban's Theories* (The Hague, 1971).

14. For evaluations of the relation between metaphor and simile, see "An Enigma: Metaphor and Simile (EIKON)," in Ricoeur's *Rule of Metaphor*, pp. 24–27. See also Monroe Beardsley's discussion of the "Literalist Theory" in *Aesthetics* (New York, 1958), p. 136. Andrew Ortony examines the communicative "processing" (in terms of predication) of simile and metaphor in "The Role of Similarity in Simile and Metaphor" in *Metaphor and Thought*, ed. Andrew Ortony (New York, 1979), pp. 186–201. Max Black's thoughts on the relation between simile and metaphor are in the section "Metaphor and Simile" of his essay "More About Metaphor" in Ortony, pp. 19–43. For one of the many arguments against identifying simile and metaphor, see Davidson, in Sacks, pp. 36–39.

15. See Ricoeur's *Rule of Metaphor*, p. 197, on the notion of metaphor as the *applying* of meaning (predicates). In formulating the "Controversion Theory," Beardsley, in *Aesthetics* (p. 142), explains the operation of metaphor as the *attribution* of connotations to denotative meaning. Philip Wheelwright, like many others, considers the mechanism of metaphor a transfer of meaning; see *Metaphor and Reality* (Bloomington, 1962), pp. 72–78. Benjamin Hrushovski conceives of metaphor as a transfer between what he postulates as the "basic unit of semantic interpretation": frames of reference; see "Poetic Metaphor and Frames of Reference," in *Poetics Today* 5 (1984): 12, 16.

16. On the notion of identity in metaphor, see Ricoeur who, in *Rule of Metaphor*, p. 26, argues against the idea that metaphor involves strict identity. See also Roger Searle, "Metaphors: Live, Dead, and Silly," in *The Play of Language*, ed. Leonard F. Dean, Walker Gibson, and Kenneth G. Wilson (New York, 1971), p. 316.

17. Donald Davidson, in his 1978 essay "What Metaphors Mean," explains that the

> simile says there is a likeness and leaves it to us to pick out some common feature or features; but metaphor does not explicitly assert a likeness, but if we accept it as a metaphor, we are again led to seek common features. . . . (In Sacks, p. 38)

18. In what could be construed as an explanation of this, Ricoeur points out that "Meta-

phor reveals the logical structure of 'the similar' because, in the metaphorical statement, 'the similar' is perceived *despite* difference, *in spite of* contradiction" (*Rule of Metaphor*, p. 196).

19. See "Metaphor and Transcendence," in Sacks, pp. 71–88. Beardsley interprets metaphorical meaning in light of the "supervenience" theory as "extraneous to, and independent of" literal meaning, and in addition "inexplicable" in terms of it. E. D. Hirsch, Jr., describes metaphor as "the making of a new identification never conceived before" and "the process of metaphor" as creating a "new verbal type"; see *Validity in Interpretation* (New Haven, 1967), p. 105.

20. Ricoeur holds that, at bottom, theories of metaphor presuppose that it operates on the level of the word (rhetoric, semiotic), on that of the sentence (semantic), or on the plane of discourse (hermeneutic). His position is that metaphorical meaning must be conceived in terms of discourse; see *Rule of Metaphor*, p. 44 and study 8, pp. 257–313.

21. For an incisive account of the prediscursive aspect of experience as the essential ground of analytical thought, see Stanley Rosen's *Limits of Analysis*. Rosen's insights into the range and limitations of analysis are considered in some detail in chapter 3 of the present study, where I take up the function of analytic discourse in the understanding of metaphor.

22. See Hrushovski's "Poetic Metaphor," p. 7.

23. Ong makes this observation in a discussion of oral history, though it is equally applicable to imaginative literature; see *Interfaces of the Word* (Ithaca, 1977), p. 74.

24. As Hrushovski discerns,

Isolating metaphor as a linguistic unit . . . [means] separating the processing of language from a reader's processing of texts, including the construction of fictional (or 'intentional') characters, settings, and 'worlds,' as projected in works of literature. ("Poetic Metaphor," p. 7)

25. Cf. Hrushovski's contention that

we must observe metaphors in literature not as static, discrete units, but as dynamic patterns, changing in the text continuum, context-sensitive, relating to specific (fictional or real) frames of reference and dependent on interpretations. ("Poetic Metaphor," p. 7)

Though his evaluation of metaphor in many ways closely parallels that put forward in this study, Hrushovski's is a semantic approach based on the unexplained notion of "metaphorical transfer."

26. *Philosophical Perspectives*, p. 26. Cf. Jacques Derrida's view (one that is influenced by semiotics and is essentially Aristotelian):

no matter how deeply buried, the link of the signifier to the signified has had both to be and to remain of natural necessity, of analogical participation, of resemblance. Metaphor has always been defined as the trope of resemblance; not simply as the resemblance between a signifier and a signified but as the resemblance between two signs, one of which designates the other. This is the most general characteristic of metaphor. . . . ("White Mythology" in *Margins of Philosophy*, trans. Alan Bass [Chicago, 1982], p. 215)

27. John Searle, *Expression and Meaning* (Cambridge, 1979).

28. See *Metaphor and Thought*, pp. 124–35.

29. *Philosophy and Phenomenological Research* 32 (1971):78–88. Yoos's perspective on

metaphor is closely allied to that presented in this study. See chapter 3, section 4, for a discussion of Yoos's approach.

30. In *The Rule of Metaphor* (p. 143), Ricoeur draws a distinction between the interaction theory as Black developed it and resemblance-predicated comparison theories. He terms the former *semantic theory* and the latter *substitution theory*. Black's definition in *Models and Metaphors* of the substitution theory is more narrow: "Any view which holds that a metaphorical expression is used in place of some equivalent *literal* expression" (p. 31).

As noted earlier, Ricoeur perceives theories of metaphor as rooted on the level of words, sentences, or discourse. The work of continental "new Rhetoric" theorists, such as Umberto Eco (in "The Scandal of Metaphor: Metaphorology and Semiotics"), is predominantly semiotic analysis and thus, as Ricoeur points out, focuses on the word as the primary unit of meaning and of semantic deviation. I follow Ricoeur's classification of semiotic approaches as variations of the substitution theory.

31. For an explanation of Richards's notion that words are "acts of the mind, " see Warren Shibles's *Analysis of Metaphor in the Light of W. M. Urban's Theories*, p. 131. In his introduction to *Metaphor: Problems and Perspectives* (Atlantic Highlands, NJ, 1982), David S. Miall explains the significance of Richards's cognitive view of metaphor in the following way:

> Words obtain meaning only from their connections with other words in a discourse. There is no standard or schematic meaning for any word: sentences are not built up out of fixed, atomic units of meaning. This claim, if true, renders unavailable some of the standard semantic procedures that might be applied to explicating metaphor. Richards, on the contrary, emphasizes what he calls the interanimation of words which makes metaphor not just a matter of verbal displacement, but a 'borrowing between and intercourse of *thoughts*, a transaction between contexts' [cf. Hrushovski]. It is the liberation into a genuinely cognitive approach which allows Richards to recognize the role of disparity in metaphor, and to suggest a view of the power of metaphor beyond the limits of words as such, or sensory images. (P. xiii)

32. George Lakoff and Mark Johnson "identify emergent categories and concepts" that metaphors effect as "experiential gestalts"; see "Conceptual Metaphor in Everyday Language," in Johnson, pp. 286–325. The essay summarizes views that Lakoff and Johnson develop at length in *Metaphors We Live By* (Chicago, 1980).

33. Black summarizes the essentials of his approach and explains modifications of his original theory in "More About Metaphor," in Ortony, pp. 28–29.

34. As noted earlier, Black in his 1977 essay asserts that it is "needlessly paradoxical, though not plainly mistaken"; yet he concludes that in

> retrospect, the intended emphasis upon 'systems,' rather than upon 'things' or 'ideas,' (as in Richards) looks like one of the chief novelties in the earlier study. (In Ortony, p. 28)

35. Note Frye's acute observation "that as we move from fictional to thematic emphasis, the element represented by the term *mythos* tends to mean increasingly 'narrative' rather than 'plot' "; see *Anatomy of Criticism* (Princeton, 1957), pp. 53, 73.

36. See Searle, in Ortony, p. 121. For a critique of Searle's speech-act analysis of metaphor on grounds that are consistent with the view of metaphor introduced in the present study, see Stephen Davies, "Truth-Values and Metaphors," *Journal of Aesthetics and Art Criticism* 42 (1984):295–97.

37. In Ortony, p. 100; cf., on the other hand, W. V. Quine's "suggestion . . . that it is nonsense, and the root of much nonsense, to speak of a linguistic component [for instance, "word meaning"] and a factual component [such as being metaphorical] in the truth of any statement"; see *From a Logical Point of View*, 2d ed. (New York, 1961), p. 42.

38. In Ortony, pp. 104–5; see Levin's challenge to Searle's critique, in Ortony, pp. 124–28.

39. *Metaphor and Reality* (Bloomington, 1962), chap. 4. For a discussion of "epiphor" in Aristotle's analysis of metaphor, see Ricoeur's *Rule of Metaphor*, pp. 17–24.

40. As Shibles explains in *An Analysis of Metaphor*, according to this perspective metaphor is "grasped immediately or intuitively before any step by step analysis" (p. 16). In this connection, see F. S. C. Northrop's distinction between "intuition" and "postulation," in *The Logic of the Sciences and the Humanities* (1947; rpt. Cleveland, 1967), pp. 82–83.

41. See *An Analysis of Metaphor*, chap. 4, n. 7, for Shibles's list of theorists who subscribe to the supervenience view.

42. See *Beyond the Letter* (London, 1979), p. 82. In his classification of metaphor theories, Scheffler relies to a great extent on Beardsley's analysis of metaphor; see *Beyond the Letter*, chap. 3, n. 3.

43. Scheffler distinguishes between emotive and intuitionistic approaches in the following way:

> The *emotive* approach lays stress upon the capacity of metaphor to evince or arouse feelings, as distinct from conveying information. Unlike the intuitionistic insistence on the power of metaphor to outstrip the cognitive range of literal expression, the emotive view emphasizes rather that metaphor goes beyond literal language in its capacity to affect feeling. (P. 87)

It is not all clear that an intuitionist such as Wheelwright, for instance, would regard as divergent from his view a theory that presumes meaning to be "emotive as well as cognitive," one that "emphasizes the emotive irreplaceability of metaphor and the resistance of its emotive meaning to formula" (*Beyond the Letter*, p. 88).

44. The interaction theory in particular—which, says Scheffler, "verges on contextualism."

45. See Ricoeur, *The Rule of Metaphor*, pp. 131–32, and Earl R. MacCormac, *A Cognitive Theory of Metaphor* (Cambridge, MA, 1985), pp. 33–34.

46. This aspect of Beardsley's position is interactionist and is open to the same objections raised against Black's theory.

47. *The Rule of Metaphor*, p. 299. Falling back on an unexplained Aristotelian assumption, Ricoeur terms this "cast into the new referential field" a "transfer."

48. In Sacks, p. 4. Cohen is indebted to John Austin's influential discrimination of "locution," "illocution," and "perlocution"; see Austin's *How to Do Things with Words*, 2d ed., ed. J. O. Urmson and Maria Sbisa (Cambridge, MA, 1975). John Searle also owes a great deal to Austin's analysis; as does Samuel Levin, who in the opening chapter of *The Semantics of Metaphor* (Baltimore, 1977) interprets Cohen as being concerned with *pragmatic* deviance. Cf. in this connection Donald Davidson (whom Cohen regards as one of the few theorists—such as Ricoeur—to have developed a theory of meaning as a basis for their postulations about metaphor), who locates his divergence with the approaches of Black, Henle, Nelson Goodman, and Beardsley in his perception of a "distinction between what words mean and what they are used to do" (in Sacks, p. 31).

49. This is precisely the approach that I argue for in the present study with respect to literary metaphor, and a theory of literary experience (expounded in chapter 2) provides the background of meaning that makes tenable the notion of metaphor as a dramatically depictive image.

50. As Hrushovski significantly discerns,

> many theories of metaphor are based on simple examples, often domesticated in language (e.g., Max Black's "man is a wolf" or John Searle's "Sally is a block of ice," which, of course, serve their own purposes well). It is not clear that such observations are transferable to more extensive and obscure instances of creative metaphor. ("Poetic Metaphor and Frames of Reference," p. 6)

In this connection, Roland Bartel notes that

> An indispensable quality of poetic metaphors is that they are inseparable from their contexts. They are organic rather than ornamental. They are so thoroughly integrated with the meaning and form of a poem that they cannot be uprooted. (*Metaphor and Symbols* [Urbana, 1983], p. 54)

See also Terence Hawkes's discussion of the shift from Aristotelian thinking about metaphor as "detachable" to Romantic approaches that

> tend to proclaim metaphor's organic relationship to language as a whole, and to lay stress on its vital functions as an expression of the faculty of Imagination. (*Metaphor* [London, 1977], p. 34)

51. Cf. Davidson's controversial contention that a metaphor has no nonliteral or "special" meaning, that it does not convey a "coded message" (in Sacks, p. 44).

52. Levin, for instance, would understand the entire poem in "phenomenal" terms, as a unique "possible" or imaginary ("poetic") world, one in which *every* figurative expression is construed literally, since "for the reader of a poem there is one single metaphor and that is the world of the poem" (*Semantics of Metaphor*, p. 132).

53. On this account, the figurative signification could not be construed to be the metaphor since it is through the transaction effected *by the metaphor* (or at least some sort of transaction constituting metaphorical meaning) that generates the figurative meaning.

54. Scheffler, who sees contextualism from this angle, remarks that

> an understanding of the context for the understanding of significant predicates, clearly requires also a grasp of the literal application of the term in question. For the metaphorical application is to be understood as attaching to things showing satisfaction of contextually important predicates with those picked out by literal application. (*Beyond the Letter*, p. 128)

55. Davidson makes this distinction to delineate just where he disagrees with the views of other theorists such as Richards, Black, and Owen Barfield; see Sacks, p. 44.

56. Hrushovski argues, for instance, that metaphor is not "a linguistic unit but a text-semantic pattern, and semantic patterns in texts cannot be identified with units of syntax" ("Poetic Metaphor," p. 7).

57. The term, made familiar by Stephen C. Pepper, refers to a "basic analogy," a process of conception that articulates a comprehensive point of view; see *World Hypotheses* (Berkeley, 1942), pp. 91–92. Cf. MacCormac's notion of "basic metaphor" in *A Cognitive Theory of Metaphor*, pp. 46–50.

58. See Hrushovski, "Poetic Metaphor and Frames of Reference, " p. 6.

59. A fascinating example of the large literature on how entire realms of experience and

evidence get overlooked or misrepresented as a result of inappropriate or inadequate theoretical models is Viktor E. Frankl's discussion of "dimensional anthropology" in his essay
"Reductionism and Nihilism," in *Beyond Reductionism*, ed. Arthur Koestler and J. R.
Smythies (New York, 1969), esp. pp. 403–07. See also Bergson's classic discussion of the
spatial and numerical reductions of duration in *Time and Free Will*, trans. F. L. Pogson
(1910; rpt. New York, 1960), esp. chap. 2.

60. Cf. Marcus B. Hester's assertion that "disagreements as to the definition of metaphor
can be settled by considering the theory of meaning of poetic metaphor." See *The Meaning
of Poetic Metaphor* (The Hague, 1967).

61. An example of the kind of theoretical difficulty inevitable in the absence of such a
consideration is when George Lakoff and Mark Johnson in "Conceptual Metaphor in Everyday Language" explain metaphorical meaning as "understanding and interpreting one
thing or experience in terms of another" (in Johnson, p. 298). "This description," as
Earl R. MacCormac objects, "could fit any semantical meaning, the association of one word
with another or the association of a word with an experience" (*A Cognitive Theory of Metaphor*, p. 59). The essence of Lakoff and Johnson's definition—"in terms of"—is left vague
and indeed remains inexplicable in the context of their approach. Max Black recognized
this same difficulty with his own theory. The question that needs to be addressed, and the
answer for which in the case of literary metaphor the present study affords a rationale, is,
What does it mean to say that metaphorical meaning is the "understanding and interpreting
of one kind of thing or experience in terms of [or "as"] another"? The perspective from
which to address this is, it seems to me, principally epistemological, for without a coherent
epistemology of metaphorical meaning, no cogent answer is possible.

62. Karl Popper lucidly summarizes Tarski's theory:

> The semantics (L_1) of an object language (L_0)—that is, the metalanguage that contains the con-
> cept "true in L_0" as a definable concept—must be *essentially richer* (of a higher order) than the
> object language (L_0).
>
> The object language L_0 may contain, as we know, its own syntax and, more especially, de-
> scriptive names of all its own expressions. But L_0 cannot, without antinomy, contain specifically
> semantic terms like *denotation, satisfaction,* or *truth*; that is, notions which relate the *names of
> the expressions* of L_0 to the *facts or objects* to which these expressions refer. (*Objective Knowledge*,
> rev. ed. [Oxford, 1979], p. 324)

63. If, for example, the whole range of unambiguously expressive human behavior were
to serve as the metalanguage, the meaning of any true statement in an object language
would be determined by the expressive behavior it manifested and elicited.

64. For a notable instance of the continental "new rhetoric" which deals with metaphor,
see the Group μ's *A General Rhetoric*, trans. Paul M. Burrell and Edgar M. Slotkin (Baltimore, 1970).

65. For a semantic approach (grounded in semiotics), see Eco's "Scandal of Metaphor,"
esp. sec. 11. Two grammatical approaches are Christina Brooke-Rose's *A Grammar of
Metaphor* (London, 1970) and Levin's "Poetry and Grammaticalness" in *Essays on the Language of Literature*, ed. Seymore Chatman and Samuel R. Levin (Boston, 1967). Fred R.
Dallmayr's observation about the linguistic perspective on experience suggests the fundamental limitation (noted by others such as Terence Hawkes) of this kind of approach to
metaphor: "As a science dealing with the a priori structures of signification, linguistics is

. . . unconcerned with human agency or experience . . ." (*Twilight of Subjectivity* [Amherst, 1981], p. 27).
    Cf. in this connection the following observation by W. Wolfgang Holdheim in an essay on "Wilhelm Worringer and the Polarity of Understanding":

> Rhetorical and linguistic schemata are reified detriti of literature and language, rigidified into pure objects of perception and description. This, of course, implies an equally pure cognitive subject who transcends the schemata, as the supreme, though unexamined norm of truth. Essential discourse does not operate on the level of such derivative abstractions, it is not an object of knowledge but is equi-original with the act of knowing itself. . . . The homology of art and knowledge is situated in the aesthetico-cognitive ground, not on the taxonomic surface. (*The Question of Textuality*, ed. William V. Spanos, Paul A. Bove, and Daniel O'Hara [Bloomington, 1982], p. 353)

66. Whitehead considers modes of "importance" an index of the relation between perspective and experience. Although at first glance modes of "importance" seem hardly determinate enough to orientate theoretical analysis, Whitehead brilliantly expounds the notion of "importance" as "a basis of our primary consciousness of quality." Whitehead indicates the link of a mode of "importance" to literature by explaining that words, which usually "indicate useful particularities," can "be employed to evoke a sense of that general character on which all importance depends," since "it is one function of great literature to evoke a vivid feeling of what lies beyond words." See *Modes of Thought* (1938; rpt. New York, 1968), chap. 1.

67. In the sense that any version of the facts is at best a likely story, all discourse is narrative and potentially literary. In this study, narrative involves the figurative *use* of language, from the single phoneme or word through the allegory and cultural myth in literary art.
    Stein Haugom Olsen argues that "literary discourse cannot be interpreted as being intended to inform" and that "judgments about the truth or falsity of literary words are . . . inappropriate." As he sees it, "literary discourse and informative discourse are two mutually exclusive classes"; see *The Structure of Literary Understanding* (Cambridge, 1978), p. 58. It is implausible, I believe, to maintain that literary experience is restricted to discourse that is not informative. Literary masterpieces like *Gulliver's Travels* and *Rasselas* were certainly written to be "interpreted as being intended to inform."
    Hayden White, in *Tropics of Discourse* (Baltimore, 1978), concerned with " 'the literature of fact' or as I have chosen to call it 'the fictions of factual representations, ' " explores "the extent to which the discourse of the historian and that of the imaginative writer overlap, resemble, or correspond with each other." White observes that although

> historians and writers of fiction may be interested in different kinds of events, both the forms of their respective discourses and their aims in writing are often the same. In addition, in my view, the technique or strategies that they use in the composition of their discourses can be shown to be substantially the same, however different they may appear on a purely surface, or dictional, level of their texts.
> Readers of histories and novels can hardly fail to be struck by their similarities. (P. 121)

68. See *The Forms of Things Unknown* (New York, 1960), p. 112, where Read distinguishes between "poetry as a primordial activity of consciousness" and "poetic thinking or myth-making."

2. Literary Experience

1. The phenomenological view of literary experience presented in this chapter and that of literary metaphor in chapter 3 derives from what Quentin Lauer identifies as a fundamental principle of phenomenological method, the "attempt to get away from speculative constructionism and to limit oneself to the data which are presented in consciousness—describing rather than explaining them." See *Phenomenology* (1958; rpt. New York, 1965), p. 1. See also "What is Phenomenology?" Maurice Merleau-Ponty, in *The Phenomenology of Perception*, trans. Colin Smith (New York, 1962), pp. vii–xvi.

In "Cassirer's Philosophy of Language" Wilbur Marshall Urban, author of *Language and Reality* (London, 1939), states explicitly what is presupposed in the present study, namely, that the understanding of language is essentially phenomenological:

> The sole entrance to the understanding of language is through meaning, for meaning is the *sine qua non* of linguistic fact. . . . the methodology of linguistic study is not that of the natural sciences but rather, for language, as for all symbolic forms, phenomenological. (In Schilpp, p. 409)

2. See Edmund Husserl, *Ideas: General Introduction to Phenomenology*, trans. W. R. Boyce Gibson (1931; rpt. New York, 1962), chap. 3. For a discussion of the life-world as a limiting concept in phenomenological thought, see "The Life-World and the Concept of Reality," Hans Blumenberg, in *Life-World and Consciousness: Essays for Aron Gurwitsch*, ed. Lester E. Embree (Evanston, 1972), pp. 425–44. Stanley Rosen in *Limits of Analysis* (New York, 1980) significantly points out that "even the phenomenological description of the life-world is a conceptual analysis of structure, and not a presentation of the world as it is" (p. 220). In view of this it should be stressed that the phenomenological perspective on literary experience developed in the present chapter, as well as the experiential account of metaphor in chapter 3 that is predicated upon it, are descriptions ("versions") and not poetic presentations ("visions") of the world as we live it, although such indeed *is* the nature of *literary experience*. In this connection see Rosen's comparison of the Platonic dialogue and Husserlian analysis, in *Limits of Analysis*, pp. 220ff.

3. C. I. Lewis, *An Analysis of Knowledge and Valuation* (LaSalle, 1946).

4. John Dewey indicates both the connection between aesthetic experience and immediacy *and* the potentially unlimited range of what can be given in awareness as immediate:

> It cannot be asserted too strongly that what is not immediate is not aesthetic. The mistake lies in supposing that only certain *special* things—those attached to the eye, ear, etc—can be qualitatively and immediately experienced.

As Dewey goes on to note, William James "showed that there is no relation so comprehensive that it may not become a matter of immediate experience." See *Art as Experience* (1934; rpt. New York, 1958), p. 119.

5. Wolfgang Iser, *The Act of Reading* (Baltimore, 1978), p. 22. Stressing the primacy of immediate, aesthetic, experience, A. N. Whitehead went as far as to declare that the "elucidation of immediate experience is sole justification for any thought; and the starting point for thought is the analytic observation of components of this experience." See *Process and Reality, Corrected Edition*, ed. David Ray Griffin and Donald W. Sherburne (New York, 1978), p. 4.

6. See Michael Polanyi's well-known study of "tacit knowledge" in "Personal Knowl-

edge," chapter 2 of *Meaning* (Chicago, 1975). See also *The Tacit Dimension* (New York, 1966).

7. Rudolph Arnheim, *Visual Thinking* (Berkeley, 1969).

8. Karl Popper might term them *adaptations*. Cf. Popper's use of this term in his discussion of the epistemological implications of biologically determined experience, in *Unended Quest*, p. 134. Tacit or prereflective (or "unconscious") epistemological adaptations are conceived in the present study as moments of cognition. In line with Arnheim's use of the term, I take "cognition" to refer to the psychophysical activity that is the necessary condition of any experience that is intelligible. Cognition could thus be said to be a function of both prediscursive and discursive modes of awareness to the degree that their deliverances are intelligible.

See also Angus Sinclair's (Kantian) view that judgment normally considered to involve interpretive operations is intrinsic in awareness per se:

> The theory that there is a fundamental difference between "awareness of . . . " and "judgment that . . ." is untenable and misleading without this qualification. There is no simple awareness of what just is, any more than there are facts which just are what they are. (*The Conditions of Knowing* [New York, 1951], p. 95)

9. See "Hermeneutics and Intellectual History," *Journal of the History of Ideas* 46 (1985):290. Stern suggests further that "Conflict among interpretations is intelligible against the background of a stable meaning. Also, a shared understanding is considered primarily a precondition rather than a result of interpretation" (p. 292). Cf., however, Rosen's assertion that as an intuitive phenomenon "perception, whether sensuous or intellectual, is neither explaining nor understanding" (*Limits of Analysis*, p. 8). See also Stephen Strasser's discussion of the primacy of understanding in *Understanding and Explanation* (Pittsburgh, 1985), sec. 9.

For a discussion (in line with the approach that I take in the present study) that probes the concepts of interpretation and understanding in terms of literary theory, see Richard E. Palmer's *Hermeneutics* (Evanston, 1969), chap. 13.

10. Benjamin Hrushovski in "An Outline of Integrational Semantics" maintains that theorists ought to "use literary texts for the observation of language phenomena and the construction of a more adequate theory of language" (*Poetics Today* 3 [1982]: 62). This contrasts sharply with views such as those of J. L. Austin, who in *How to Do Things with Words* asserts that with respect to literary language, "performative utterances" are "*in a peculiar way* hollow or void. . . . Language in such circumstances is in special ways— intelligibly—used not seriously, but in ways parasitic upon its normal use" (quoted in Iser, p. 58).

11. Analytic concepts, theories, and strategies may be primitive in their own right. In this connection see Ernest Nagel's distinction between "experiential" and "theoretical" primitives in "The Meaning of Reduction in the Natural Sciences" (in Danto and Morgenbesser, pp. 299–300).

12. In his *Logic of the Sciences and the Humanities*, F. S. C. Northrop conceives this widely noted dichotomy of direct (i. e., prediscursive or antepredicative) and mediated (i.e., discursive or structural) modes of consciousness that has appeared in Western thinking since the time of the pre-Socratics as "immediately apprehended fact" and "described fact."

See chapter 3 of Northrop's work for a discussion of the distinction between the deliverances of these two kinds of experience. Cf. also Bergson's discussion of the "deep distinction" between intuitive and analytical ways of knowing in "Introduction to Metaphysics," *The Creative Mind*, trans. Maybelle L. Andison (New York, 1946), chap. 6. W. Wolfgang Holdheim in his essay "Wilhelm Worringer and the Polarity of Understanding" casts this "deep distinction" as a perennial struggle between "empathy" in the form of historical understanding viewed (somewhat after the manner of Collingwood) as the "imaginative recreation of human experience, expressed in the narrative process," and the effort "to subject even history . . . to the theoretical mode of knowledge by reducing phenomena to abstract universal laws" (in Spanos, p. 353). Holdheim explains that this

> conflict in historical epistemology has been going on for many generations and shows no signs of abating. . . . Positivist explanation and structuralist reduction are pitted against hermeneutic comprehension, the abstract against the concrete. Epistemologically, "concrete" refers to . . . "to congeal" or (more originally) "to grow together" . . . various strands of occurrence temporarily grow together, standing in relief . . . as meaningful organic configurations called "events." Theoretical knowledge works through *construction* of the abstract, hermeneutic comprehension through *Heivorhebung* [the standing in relief] of the concrete. Theoretical abstraction is obtained by an *application* of method that is mechanical, manipulatory [Cf. the formulaic approaches to metaphor]. . . . Hermeneutic empathy is based on a temporal concrescence, and accretion of experience is its aim. (P. 354)

Holdheim's insightful discussion provides a rationale for an approach such as that undertaken in the present inquiry, one that argues for the recognition of the primacy of the prediscursive dimension of experience in metaphorical meaning. In the context of literary experience, however, what Holdheim calls "temporal" concrescence might more accurately be termed *thematic* concrescence. On the other hand, what he refers to as "hermeneutic empathy" corresponds to the notion of "enactive envisagement" introduced near the end of section 2 of the present chapter.

Concerned specifically with phenomenological epistemology, Maurice Merleau-Ponty explains that analysis (Holdheim's "positivist explanation and structuralist reduction") reconstructs rather than merely elucidates experience; in other words, description (including that which is phenomenological) reformulates what is immediately apprehended. Merleau-Ponty is reacting against the characteristic analytic fallacy of identifying the *form* of description with what is being described, something that is rooted, as Fred R. Dallmayr (quoting Merleau-Ponty) observes, in the " 'philosophy of reflection' (dating back to Descartes), with its proclivity to treat perception as 'the thought of perceiving' and the perceived world as 'a thing thought' " (*Twilight of Subjectivity*, p. 104).

13. In his essay on "Cassirer, Neo-Kantianism, and Phenomenology," Fritz Kaufmann points out that "To the phenomenological there are no pre-established 'transcendental facts' " (in Schilpp, p. 806). That is to say, no analytic categories or forms are in any sense prior to, prerequisites of, experience.

14. The vivacity and concreteness of "sense meaning" is a natural medium of abstract conceptual data since sense meaning does not actually denote anything. C. I. Lewis in *An Analysis of Knowledge and Valuation* lucidly explains:

> Sense meaning obviously could not be identified with denotation, and is no wise dependent upon existence of what is meant. . . . Sense meaning as criterion, is independent of any question of

existence or non-existence of that to which the criterion applies. The fact that there are no centaurs has no bearing on the meaningfulness of "centaur". . . . Comprehension and sense meaning are coterminous; but denotation and sense meaning are not. (P. 137)

15. Frye reasserts here an age-old humanistic insight, one that informs, for example, Sir Philip Sidney's *Defence of Poesie* (1595). In the first of the two passages cited below, Sidney comments on the sensuous imagery that poets (by which he means literary artists generally) employ to communicate ideas. The second is an observation on how, through poetic imagery, the poet humanizes the natural world.

[W]hatsoever the *Philosopher* saith should be done, [the poet] gives a perfect picture of it by some one, by who he presupposeth it was done, so as he coupleth the generall notion with the particuler example. A perfect picture I say, for hee yeeldeth to the powers of the minde an image of that whereof the *Philosopher* bestoweth but a wordish description, which doth neither strike, pearce, nor possesse the sight of the soule so much, as that other doth. (*Complete Works*, vol. 3, p. 14)

Onely the Poet . . . lifted up with the vigor of his own invention, doth grow in effect into another nature: in making things either better than Nature bringeth foorth, or quite a new, formes such as never were in nature: as the Herodes, Demigods, Cyclops, Chymeras, Furies, and such like; so as he goeth hand in hand with nature, not enclosed within the narrow warrant of her gifts, but freely ranging within the Zodiack of his owne wit. (P. 8)

16. Recall that Arnheim alludes to a "continuous field" in which "the components of intuitive processes interact." He contrasts this with analytical "intellectual operations" that he conceives as a linear assemblage, as a "stepwise connection between fixed entities" (*Visual Thinking*, p. 235). Cf. in this connection William James's observations on the givenness of sensations and that of (analytic) terms, in *A Pluralistic Universe*, ed. Frederick Burkhardt, Fredson Bowers, and Ignas K. Skrupskelis (Cambridge, MA, 1977), pp. 126–27.

17. Jean-Paul Sartre, *Literature and Existentialism*, trans. Bernard Frechtman (New York, 1964).

18. In this connection see Paul Ricoeur's discussion of "emplotment" in *Time and Narrative*, vol. 1, trans. Kathleen McLaughlin and David Pellauer (Chicago, 1984), pp. 161–68.

19. Cf. Nietzsche's characterization of "literary decadence" that he sees as informing approaches to literature for which

The word becomes sovereign and leaps out of the sentence, the sentence reaches out and obscures the meaning of the page, and the page comes to life at the expense of the whole—the whole is no longer a whole. This, however, is the simile of every style of decadence: every time there is an anarchy of atoms. (Quoted in Kaufmann's *Nietzsche*, p. 73)

20. For a detailed critique of Langer's views on literary experience, see Phillip A. Stambovsky, "The Depictive Image: Metaphor and Literary Experience." Ph. D. diss. University of Massachusetts, 1987, pp. 96–100.

21. Sartre, in the language of phenomenological philosophy, would term this "the intentional attitude of conscious apprehension"; see *Essays in Existentialism*, p. 265.

22. To assert that what appears fixed does so only relative to perceived changes is not

more compelling logically than to claim that what seems passing appears so only from a perspective that fails to recognize that "form" (from what might be called a 4-D viewpoint) includes temporality and flux (or transition) as elements of its definition. Giambattista Vico made somewhat the same point in the context of his analysis of metaphor (which, in the mode of personification, he identifies with the fable—"a fable in brief"). Donald Philip Verene explains that for Vico "fable or metaphor is true speech because it . . . brings forth the *is* as the given of human mentality. This given is something made" (*Vico's Science of Imagination* [Ithaca, 1981], p. 83).

23. Käte Hamburger, *The Logic of Literature*, 2d ed., trans. Marilyn J. Rose (Bloomington, 1973).

24. Ernst Cassirer, *Symbol, Myth, and Culture*, ed. Donald Phillip Verene (New Haven, 1979).

25. Arthur F. Kinney makes it clear that William Faulkner was notably sensitive to this fact:

Time, Faulkner once declared, does not exist "in the momentary avatars of individual people"; he might have said the same for space. Neither is actual nor reportorial but imaginatively and individually constructed. (*Faulkner's Narrative Poetics* [Amherst, 1978] p. 7)

26. Explaining extension as a moment of experience that is more primitive than, yet characteristic of, space and time, A. N. Whitehead sees extension in its pure form ("apart from its spatialization and temporalization") as

that general scheme of relationships providing the capacity that many objects can be welded into the real unity of one experience. . . . These extensive relationships are more fundamental than their more special spatial and temporal relationships. (*Process and Reality*, p. 67)

As the presentational immediacy of literary experience is, conceptually speaking, thematically structured, it is pertinent to note as an addendum to the passage cited Whitehead's comment that the "general scheme of relationships corresponds to thematic content." See *Process and Reality*, part IV for Whitehead's "Theory of Extension."

27. In this connection, see Langer's discussion of presentational symbolism in *Philosophy in a New Key*, 3d ed. (Cambridge, MA, 1957), chap. 4.

The aesthetically immediate in literary experience is dramatically present for awareness and may be distinguished from data that are immediate in other ways as that which has *presence*. See Guiseppina Moneta's discussion of the phenomenology of presentational awareness in "The Foundation of Predicative Experience and the Spontaneity of Consciousness" (in Embree, pp. 171–90).

28. See *Symbolism* (1927; rpt. New York, 1959), chap. 1, and *Process and Reality*, part 2, chap. 8 and part 4, chap. 4. A useful introduction to *Process and Reality* is Donald W. Sherburne's *Key to Whitehead's PROCESS AND REALITY* (1966; rpt. Bloomington, 1975). Other helpful explications of Whitehead's philosophical system include Elizabeth M. Kraus, *The Metaphysics of Experience* (New York, 1979); Ivor Leclerc, *Whitehead's Metaphysics* (Bloomington, 1975); and A. H. Johnson, *Whitehead's Theory of Reality* (1952; rpt. New York, 1962). For a trenchant critique of Whitehead's philosophical system (especially his views on presentational immediacy and causal efficacy), see Stephen David Ross, *Perspective in Whitehead's Metaphysics* (Albany, 1983).

29. This applies, of course, in the special case of the presentational immediacy of lit-

erary experience. To anticipate somewhat, the valuation "integrated" with presentational literary experience is *dramatic* in nature.

30. For Whitehead's discussion of contemporaneousness, see *Process and Reality*, pp. 61–62, 123.

31. As he explains in *Symbolism*,

> By "presentational immediacy" I mean what is usually termed "sense-perception." But I am using the former term under limitations and extensions which are foreign to the common use of the latter term. (P. 21)

This passage exemplifies Whitehead's practice of employing common terms (other examples include his use of "feeling," "enjoyment," and "satisfaction") to express comprehensive philosophical ideas.

32. C. I. Lewis not only finds valuation inherent in presentational immediacy ("direct experience"), he points to a "quality of signification" that is recognized as such in the light of formal analysis and that has its source in the prereflective "value-character of presentations." Lewis's observations can been seen as a succinct account of how presentational data are intelligible on the prediscursive (phenomenological) plane of literary experience:

> Not only do value-apprehensions in direct experience tend to characterize specifically those items which distinguish themselves as presentations, but it is those value-qualities which thus attach to presentation which—like the presentations themselves—tend to acquire a sign function. It is such value-character of presentations in which our deliberate interpretations find a significance of value in objects; and they already appear as possessing such a quality of signification in advance of any act of reflection or interpretation. (*Analysis of Knowledge and Valuation*, p. 425)

33. For Whitehead's views on valuation, see *Process and Reality*, pp. 240–41.

34. See the discussion of "solidarity" in *Process and Reality*, pp. 40, 66. Whitehead acknowledges borrowing his use of the term from Samuel Alexander. Cf. C. I. Lewis's statement about the relevance of context to the value-quality that characterizes presentational data:

> although the value-quality . . . directly characterizing a presentation . . . has the same character of immediate datum as does the presentation itself, this *value-quality is not simply a function of the presentation, but tends to be determined in some part by the relation of that presentation to the context of it*. (*Analysis of Knowledge and Valuation*, p. 426)

35. Cf. David Norton's observation that "All experiential facts of an organism embody the point of view of the organism." See *Personal Destinies* (Princeton, 1976), p. 249.

36. This implies that for literary experience textual meaning is not wholly a subjective affair, nor is it (*pace* Stanley Fish) completely a matter of communal, if tacit, consensus. Textual meaning is objective to the extent that readers conform in some determinable way to the formal completeness of a text. This assertion is supported in principle by Whitehead's observation that "actual things are *objectively* in our experience and formally existing in their own completeness" (*Symbolism*, p. 25).

The concept of *conformation* employed here and that of literary experience as an activity find support in Ernst Cassirer's observations on the way "artistic imagination" communicates through art objects that are not perceived or received in a passive way; we have to construct, to build up these forms [of presentational experience] in order to be aware of them, to see and feel them. This dynamic aspect gives to the static material aspect a new tinge and a new significance. All our passive states are not turned into active energies: the forms that I behold are not only my states, but my acts. (*Symbol, Myth, and Culture* [New Haven, 1979], p. 215)

Distinguishing between "cerebration" and "thinking" (analytic thought and perceptual cognition) in a remark on philosophic humility before the actualities of aesthetic experience, William Barrett describes the process of what is understood in the present work as "conformation" in literary experience: "He [the philosopher] cannot cerebrate but he must think—which means to let the work of art be what it is and follow it in its own terms" (*Time of Need*, p. 9).

37. See *Personal Destinies*, pp. 249, 268–69, 276–77.

38. This is confirmed by Whitehead's assertion in *Process and Reality* that "When human experience is in question, 'perception' almost always means 'perception in the mixed mode of symbolic reference' " (p. 168).

39. See Cassirer's *Philosophy of Symbolic Forms*, trans. Ralph Manheim, 3 vols. (New Haven, 1955–57) and his succinct summary of this philosophy, *Essay on Man* (1944; rpt. New Haven, 1976), esp. chap. 2. For a penetrating analysis of Cassirer's notion of "symbolic form," see Robert S. Hartman, "Cassirer's Philosophy of Symbolic Forms" in *The Philosophy of Ernst Cassirer*, ed. Paul Arthur Schilpp (La Salle, 1949), pp. 289–333. See also Nelson Goodman's influential application of Cassirer's concept in *Ways of Worldmaking* (Indianapolis, 1981), especially chap. 1.

40. Frye in *Fables of Identity* (New York, 1963) makes virtually the same point when he asserts that

What we are conscious of in direct literary experience is rather [than phonemes or separate words and images] a series of larger groupings, events, and scenes that make up what we call the story. (P. 22)

If "as they" replaced the relative pronoun "that" in this statement, Frye's observation would be more faithful to the processive character of literary experience.

41. Citations are from the 1974 Bantam edition. Una Allis considers how the conceptually articulated themes of the Chautauqua fit into the narrative format of the story in her essay "*Zen and the Art of Motorcycle Maintenance,*" in *Critical Quarterly* 20 (1978): 33–41.

42. Conceived as a literary genre, the literature of "therapeutic remembering"includes such other first-person narratives as Lawrence Sterne's *Tristram Shandy*, Melville's "Bartleby the Scrivener," Faulkner's *Absalom, Absalom!* and Vonnegut's *Slaughterhouse-Five*.

43. In this connection see Frye's discussion of how the literary artist uses "ideas" as "thought forms or conceptual myths" for aesthetic ends in *Fables of Identity*, p. 57.

44. The term is from Erik Erikson's eight-stage theory of psychosocial development. See Erikson's *Childhood and Society*, 2d ed. (New York, 1963), chap. 7 and *Identity and the Life Cycle* (1959; rpt. New York, 1980).

45. As Stanley Rosen points out, "theory construction is possible only on the basis of intuition, and further . . . analytical thinking is saturated with intuition at each step" (*Limits of Analysis*, p. 18). See Rosen's discerning discussion of intuition and its relation to conceptual thinking in chapter 1 of *Limits*.

George Santayana cogently defends the view that poetry is instinct with concepts, or "theory" in "Poetry and Philosophy," in *Little Essays; Drawn from the Writings of George Santayana*, ed. Logan Pearsall Smith and George Santayana [New York, 1920], p. 143.

46. Intuition in this sense could be thought of as "existence taken to the second power." Experience—the sense of existence—intensified exponentially in this way is rendered dramatically in literary art that depicts the telling of the story as *itself* part of a narrative process that constitutes the story of the teller. Literature such as the works cited in note 42 exemplify this complex kind of depiction, which as the heart of literary metaphor I term "significant depiction" (see chap. 3, sec. 3).

47. The Jesuit thinker Bernard J. F. Lonergan's explanation of the function of art in aesthetic apprehension is particularly germane in this connection. A work of art, argues Lonergan, operates through aesthetic perception in such a way as

> to mean, to convey, to import something that is to be reached, not through science or philosophy, but through a participation and, in some fashion, reenactment of the artist's inspiration and intension. (*Insight*, p. 185)

Maurice Merleau-Ponty is in concurrence with Lonergan's statement when he notes that "all communication supposes in the listener a creative re-enactment of what is heard" (*Essential Writings*, p. 372). Sartre is at variance with this view in that he does not admit reading to be "re-invention" of any sort, but rather a "directed creation," potentiated by the writer and that finds its "fulfillment only in reading." Sartre too is thus acutely aware of the communicative heart of aesthetic realization, stating in *What is Literature?* that "Art exists only for and through other people" (quoted in Iser, p. 108).

Nelson Goodman notes that "Psychologists and linguists have stressed the ubiquitous participation of action in perception in general, the early and extensive use of gestural, or enactive symbols, and the role of such symbols in cognitive development" (*Languages of Art*, p. 62).

48. It is in this sense that the drama inherent in the experience of fiction and poetry reveals it as a bona fide, enactively mythic form of consciousness. As Jerome Bruner has discerned, "The myth as a work of art has as its principal form the shape of drama" ("Myth and Identity" in Murray, p. 286). Wolfgang Iser links the participative aspect of literary experience to the cathartic satisfaction that literature (like drama and ceremony) potentially affords. See *The Act of Reading* (Baltimore, 1978), p. 78.

49. As Martin Foss observes: "imitation . . . is only a symbolic reduction of similarity, comparison and repetition." See his insightful, although often neglected, *Symbol and Metaphor in Human Experience* (Princeton, 1949), p. 89.

50. In *After the New Criticism* (Chicago, 1980) Frank Lentricchia criticizes Frye's "heavy reliance on a subject-object model drawn from nineteenth-century science and nineteenth-century theories of interpretation . . . " (p. 10).

Stanley Rosen identifies the distinction between subject and object as a modern derivative of the classical split of knower and known, a dichotomy that does not admit of the possibility of the knower's critical, self-conscious awareness of the process by which his coming to know conditions what is known. Rosen explains that this problematic dichotomy at the heart of the Western rationalist tradition "underlies the subject-predicate distinction [and hence the analyticity] of grammar and logic," and that when it is employed to rationalize experience (and in so doing delimit the intelligible) outside realms of high abstraction it generates "paradoxes, antinomines, and contradictions which, when we discover them, we regard as constituting the boundaries of intelligibility" (*G . W . F . Hegel* [New Haven, 1974], p. xvii). This situation is manifest in the inability of proponents of grammatic, semiotic, or mythic form, despite their own virtuosic ability to rationalize a literary work within the context of their particular universe of discourse, to explain in terms of their own closed modes of rationality the reason for privileging their particular approaches to literary art other than that alternative views can be proven wanting. See in this connection Lentricchia's critique of Frye's mythic schema in *After the New Criticism*, p. 34.

Cf. Richard E. Palmer's comment in "On Transcending the Subject-Object Schema":

> The leading challenge to interpretation in America today [1969] is to transcend the subject-object schema (through which the work tends to be placed at a distance from the interpreter as an object of analysis). Phenomenology opens the way to meet this challenge. (*Hermeneutics* [Evanston, 1969], p. 246)

Palmer cites the thinking of Gadamer, Sartre, Blanchot, Ricoeur, Merleau-Ponty and others as affording significant alternatives to approaches that presuppose the subject-object dichotomy.

51. Cf. Mihai Spariosu, ed., *Mimesis in Contemporary Theory: An Interdisciplinary Approach, Volume II: The Literary and Philosophical Debate* (Philadelphia, 1984), p. iii. This understanding of mimesis diverges from the standard acceptation of the term. As Spariosu notes, "In contemporary literary theory . . . mimesis has, at least in Anglo-American and French traditions, preserved its Platonic form almost intact . . . " (p. xviii).

For a succinct discussion of the evolution of the concept of "mimesis," see W. Tatarkiewicz's essay "Mimesis," in the *Dictionary of the History of Ideas*, ed. Philip P. Wiener (New York, 1973), vol. III, pp. 225–30. Also see Walter Kaufmann's criticism of "imitation" as an adequate translation of the Greek *mimesis*, in *Tragedy and Philosophy* (Garden City, 1968), chap. 2, sec. 9. Cf. Ricoeur's assertion in the first volume of *Time and Narrative* that "If we continue to translate mimesis by 'imitation,' we have to understand something completely contrary to a copy of some preexisting reality and speak instead of creative 'imitation' "(p. 45).

52. The reader thus in Iser's words "participates in producing the meaning" (*The Act of Reading*, p. 79) of the text. Cf. Sartre's explanation in *What is Literature?* of literary art as a communicative effort:

> When a work is produced, the creative act is only an incomplete, abstract impulse; if the author existed all on his own, he could write as much as he liked, but his work would never see the light of day as an object. . . . The process of writing, however, includes as a dialectic correlative the process of reading, and these two interdependent acts require two differently active people. The combined efforts of author and reader bring into being the concrete and imaginary object which is the work of the mind. Art exists only for and through other people. (Quoted in Iser, p. 108)

See also Charles Newman's critique of a postmodern literature that leaves us "surrounded by unfinished masterpieces—unfinished by the reader" (*The Post-Modern Aura* [Evanston, 1986], p. 92).

53. Cf. James M. Edie's assertion that "Enactment . . . is always . . . something sacred and liturgical, a rite. " This supports the contention that the mimesis of literary expe-

rience is the phenomenological expression of enactive envisagement. See Edie's "Appearance and Reality: An Essay on the Philosophy of the Theatre," *Philosophy and Literature* 4 (1980):3–17.

54. Postulating a *correlative* evolution of presentational data vis-à-vis demonstrable textual meaning avoids the reductionism that Geoffrey Hartman finds in semiotic positivists whom he sees as guilty of "an intellectual imperialism which degrades every phenomenon into a sign" ("Social Sciences and the Humanities," in *Easy Pieces* [New York, 1985], p. 171). A mode of consciousness, and so a processive actuality, literary experience is more than a mere concatenation of inwardly represented "sounds and imagery."
Cf. Iser's notion of *realization* in *The Act of Reading*, p. 68.

55. Charles Morris's assessment in *Signification and Significance* (Cambridge, MA, 1964) of the role of language in the communication of values lends credence to the contention that language apprehended purely as a vehicle of literary meaning (as it is in literary experience) communicates intuitive symbols (i.e., aesthetic values) phenomenologically, with the concrete immediacy of sense perception. As Morris puts it, "a sign portrays values mediately, while the sign-vehicle presents the same values immediately" (p. 72).

56. Cf. Cassirer's earlier analysis of mythical consciousness and perceptual awareness in *The Philosophy of Symbolic Forms*, vol. 3, p. 61.
In his *Logic of the Humanities*, trans. Clarence Smith Howe (New Haven, 1961), Cassirer maintains that the "root of myth . . . is no other thing than perception of expression" (p. 94). This observation ties in with C. I. Lewis's remark, cited at the beginning of the present chapter, about the relation between expressive statements and phenomenological experience (the aesthetic modality of perceptual awareness). Cf. Cassirer's further statement that "Primacy of expression-perception over thing-perception is what characterizes the mythical world-view" (p. 94).

57. Emerson here anticipates William James's integration of the mental image with the stream of consciousness. See the second chapter of his *Psychology: The Briefer Course*, ed. Gordon Allport (New York, 1961).

58. This is in line with Wayne Booth's view that "the worst pedagogical disaster that could befall any student of *Emma*, or *Moby-Dick* or a poem by Yeats would be the conviction that what I or any other critic has to say about it is as important as the encounter with, the experience of, the possession by, the work itself—whatever can be made of it" ("Pluralism in the Classroom," *Critical Inquiry* 12 [1986]: 474).

3. *Literary Metaphor*

1. Theodore Ziolkowski, *Disenchanted Images: A Literary Iconology* (Princeton, 1977).
2. The noted British physician and cognitive scientist Jonathan Miller makes an acute observation that suggests the cognitive limits of strictly visual imagery:

> The fact that one can dream of something without its necessarily looking like what one knows it to be means that there is at least one class of mental images whose members have what pictures and photographs do not, namely, intrinsic propositional content. ("The Mind's Eye and the Human Eye," *Daedalus* 114.4 [1985]: 198)

3. Cf. Arnheim's discussion of generic images, what he calls "pure shapes," as they relate to perceptual experience, in *Visual Thinking* (Berkeley, 1969), chap. 12.

4. Jean-Paul Sartre, *Psychology of Imagination* (Secaucus, n.d.).

5. This view could be traced to Cassirer's frequently criticized notion that mythic thinking is more primitive, on a lower plane of consciousness, than rational, scientific thinking.

6. Ernst Cassirer, *Phenomenology of Knowledge*, trans. Ralph Manheim (New Haven, 1957).

7. Volumes 23 and 24 of *The Novels and Tales of Henry James*, New York ed. (New York, 1909). Page citations refer to this edition.

8. James elsewhere describes Verver as "a slightly stale person, deprived of the general prerogative of presence" (vol. 1, p. 169).

9. An indefinite number of types of patterned relationships are legitimately ascribable to the "family coach" image, indeed to any image, and it should be clear that no structuralist claim is being made here about the universality or primordiality of any given structural configuration. The presentational form, the experiential structure, of the depictive rendering of those relationships is a form of *reason* in the Latin sense of ratio (shared also by the Greek *logos*) as "relation" or "order." See Brand Blandshard on "form" and the noetic awareness (what he would call "intelligence") that apprehends "the order and relations" of things, in *Reason and Analysis* (La Salle, 1964), p. 55.

10. The depiction of interpersonal and epistemological events in the thumbnail fable of the metaphor (which as such is functionally analogous in drama to the play-within-the-play) was first explored by Giambattista Vico. See n. 9 of the Introduction.

11. *The Philosophy of Symbolic Forms*, vol. 1, p. 319.

12. *Complete Poems*, ed. Thomas H. Johnson (Boston, 1960), pp. 496–97.

13. See Phillip A. Stambovsky, "Emily Dickinson's 'The Last Night That She Lived': Explorations of a Witnessing Spirit," *Concerning Poetry* 19 (1986): 87–93.

14. See chap. 1, n. 48, for references to analyses relating metaphorical meaning to the way we use words. Cf. Marcus B. Hester's agreement with Wittgenstein that "the meaning of a word is its use. Signs have no intrinsic meaning, but are given meaning by being linked to public contexts by use." *The Meaning of Poetic Metaphor* (The Hague, 1967), p. 68.

15. See *Metaphor and Reality* (Bloomington, 1962), chap. 4.

16. An exception would be a case such as that where, say "Man is a wolf," because it is so often cited in connection with Max Black's interaction theory, is apprehended as presenting some aspect of Black's view but is used in the context of an *opposing* theory as an implicit critique of Black's approach.

17. See Lakoff and Johnson's explanation of the experiential basis of metaphor in their criticism of the objectivist approach that attempts to "structure a situation" (i.e., the existential context of metaphor) in terms of independently conceived sets of mutually consistent metaphors; in *Metaphors We Live By* (Chicago, 1980), chap. 27.

18. Nelson Goodman, *Ways of Worldmaking* (Indianapolis, 1978).

19. Wilbur Marshall Urban, *Language and Reality* (1939; rpt. New York, 1971).

20. Ricoeur explains that one of the points he "tried to demonstrate in *The Rule of Metaphor* [is] that language's capacity for reference is not exhausted by descriptive discourse and that poetic works referred to the world in their own specific way, that of metaphorical reference." See *The Rule of Metaphor*, pp. 216–56.

21. As I have argued, depiction in literary experience can be understood to include non-picturable renderings. Such depiction parallels visual experience in its incorporation of discrete entities that are of varying spatial, temporal, or qualitative proximities to each other into the uniformly immediate field of presentational awareness. The *OED* sanctions an acceptation of "depict" beyond the merely visual, namely, "to portray, *delineate, figure anyhow*" (emphasis added).

22. Any tropological typology that holds the words "like" and "as" essential in distinguishing simile from other figures of speech is basically flawed. Tropes such as metonymy are not determined by any particular words, whether overt or "submerged." The inconsistency of the principle of discrimination between tropes—with some figures, like simile and hendiadys, considered tied to specific words and others not—reveals confusion as to just what a trope actually is: a function of words, or cognition, or of some combination of both. Cf. Philip Wheelwright's virtual rejection of the standard distinction between metaphor and simile, in *Metaphor and Reality*, p. 71; and Martin Foss's earlier criticism of the distinction, in *Symbol and Metaphor in Human Experience* (Princeton, 1949), pp. 53–57.

23. Marcus B. Hester, *The Meaning of Poetic Metaphor* (The Hague, 1967).

24. In "The Mind's Eye and the Human Eye" Jonathan Miller suggests the inadequacies of the metaphor of *seeing* with respect to the elucidation of other forms of experience:

> leaving aside the peculiar resources of tense, metaphor, irony, and indirect speech, for which
> . . . there are not conceivable counterparts in illustration, the experience of *visualizing* something as the result of reading a *description* of it is altogether different from *seeing* it in the form of
> an actual picture. (*Daedalus* 114.4 [1985]:186.

25. See p. 30, chap. 1, sec. 3, for Israel Scheffler's similar objections to Paul Henle's iconic signification theory.

26. The problem that the issue of "image poor" tenors and vehicles in metaphor poses for Hester's theory betrays his reliance on a concept of the image that is tied exclusively to sensuous, as opposed to intellectual, intuition. Hester's view generates difficulties such as the following, pointed out by Mark Johnson in the introduction of *Philosophical Perspectives on Metaphor* (Minneapolis, 1981):

> From the observation that some poetic metaphors involve images, we cannot conclude either
> that all poetic metaphors are necessarily imagistic or that the images are always necessary for
> one's comprehension. (P. 30)

27. Given the sense that the experience of metaphor does not necessarily involve any awareness of analogy, likeness, comparison, or (contrary to iconic signification views), symbol—transfer might well be included. See Yoos's critique of Paul Henle's theory, in "A Phenomenological Look," p. 85.

28. Richard Rorty concisely summarizes the role of analysis as it is understood in the present study when he comments in *Philosophy and the Mirror of Nature* (Princeton, 1979) that "We will be epistemological [as opposed to hermeneutical] where we understand perfectly well what is happening but want to codify it in order to extend, or strengthen, or teach, or 'ground' it" (p. 321).

29. "A Phenomenological Look," p. 84. In *On Metaphor* (Chicago, 1978) Donald Davidson argues persuasively in "What Metaphors Mean" for a literalist approach to metaphor. See, however, Max Black's trenchant "Reply," pp. 181–92. See also Stephen Davies,

"Truth-Value and Metaphor," *Journal of Aesthetics and Art Criticism* 42 (1984):291–302; and David Novitz, "Metaphor, Derrida, and Davidson," *Journal of Aesthetics and Art Criticism* 44 (1985):101–14.

30. Yoos takes Beardsley's verbal-opposition theory to task on this point. He also criticizes Henle's iconic signification theory along similar lines, contending that "in our awareness of metaphor there is no conscious awareness of *symbol* to justify Henle's account" ("A Phenomenological Look at Metaphor," p. 85). For Henle's version of the story, see his "Metaphor," in Johnson, pp. 83–104.

31. Robert Scholes, *Textual Power* (New Haven, 1985).

32. This is to argue that the literary work as it is read has a privileged status over any interpretive approach. Charles Newman in *The Post-Modern Aura* (Evanston, 1985) reminds us that

> While fascinating in itself, criticism simply does not create the aesthetic consciousness which it proposes to examine. Yet when criticism does penetrate *just far enough* into non-discursive experience, there is often the realization that there *are* language acts which place the critic's honest worry, restraint and scrupulousness in a severely reduced perspective. (P. 122)

33. See "Différance" in *Margins of Philosophy*, trans. Alan Bass (Chicago, 1982), pp. 1–27. For a historically grounded summary explication of this seminal term in Derrida's thought, see *Untying the Text*, ed. Richard Young (Boston, 1981), pp. 15–18.

34. See in this connection philosopher Don Ihde's discussion of the Anglo-American tradition in philosophy, a "dominantly designative" form that "founds its architectonic upon the declarative, predicating statement . . ." ("Phenomenology, 'Metaphor-Metaphysics' and the Text," in *Consequences of Phenomenology* [Albany, 1986], p. 68).

35. Paraphrasing Rosen's statement helps to underscore the fundamental difficulty of theories that endeavor to explain metaphor as an assemblage of juxtaposed or interactive components: To say that in metaphor p is understood (or viewed) *as* S by means of interaction, transference, supervenience, or comparison of meaning is not to explain (other than by appeal to circular reasoning) what "interaction," "transference," "supervenience," "comparison," or "as" means. This problem of the meaning of metaphorical meaning discussed at the conclusion of the opening chapter is, as I indicated, the point of departure for the conception of literary metaphor introduced in the present study.

36. In an earlier treatise Rosen links what he calls the " 'invisibility' of logical convention or formal structure" to "the traditional problem of the separation of a substance from its attributes" (*G. W. F. Hegel: An Introduction to the Science of Wisdom* [New Haven, 1974], p. 245). See Rosen's incisive analysis of "Whole and Parts," in *Hegel*, pp. 35–43.

37. Paul Ricoeur in "The Metaphorical Process as Cognition, Imagination and Feeling" goes so far as to consider metaphoric depiction "the functioning of the intuitive grasp of predicative connection" (in Sacks, p. 149).

38. Rosen points out that always "There is a non-discursive *context of analysis*" (*Limits of Analysis* [New York, 1980], p. 26).

39. The approach to metaphor as a depictive image might well be characterized as a contextual or *occasionalist* theory in that it assumes that words acquire determinate meaning only "in some actual or imagined occasion of use." See E. D. Hirsch, Jr., "On Theories and Metaphors," *New Literary History* 18 (1985):53.

40. I borrow the term from Ricoeur, who in the first volume of *Time and Narrative* ex-

plains emplotment as a "configurational act" that in "extracting a configuration from a succession" effects

> a mixed intelligibility between what has been called the point, theme, or thought of a story, and the intuitive presentation of circumstances, characters, episodes, and changes of fortune that make up the denouement. In this way we may speak of a schematization of the narrative function. (p. 68)

41. Quoted by Karsten Harries, in Sacks, p. 84.

BIBLIOGRAPHY

Adams, Hazard. *Philosophy of the Literary Symbolic*. Tallahassee, 1983.

Aiken, Henry David. "Some Notes Concerning the Aesthetic and the Cognitive." *Journal of Aesthetics and Art Criticism* 13 (1955): 390–91.

Aldrich, Virgil. "Pictorial Meaning, Picture Thinking, and Wittgenstein's Theory of Aspects." In *Essays on Metaphor*, 93–103. *See* Shibles.

Allis, Una. "Zen and the Art of Motorcycle Maintenance." *Critical Inquiry* 20 (1978): 33–41.

Alston, William P. *Philosophy of Language*. Englewood Cliffs, 1964.

Ankersmit, F. R. *Narrative Logic*. The Hague, 1983.

Aristotle. *The Works of Aristotle*. Ed. W. D. Ross. Oxford, 1924. Vol. 11.

Arnheim, Rudolph. *Visual Thinking*. Berkeley, 1969.

Austin, J. L. *How to Do Things with Words*. Ed. J. O. Urmson. Cambridge, MA, 1962.

Barrett, William. *Time of Need: Forms of Imagination in the Twentieth Century*. New York, 1973.

Barzun, Jacques. *A Stroll with William James*. Chicago, 1984.

Beardsley, Monroe C. *Aesthetics: Problems in the Philosophy of Criticism*. New York, 1958.

———. "The Metaphorical Twist." In *Philosophical Perspectives on Metaphor*, 105–22. *See* Mark Johnson.

Bergmann, Merrie. "Metaphorical Assertions." *The Philosophical Review* 91(1982): 229–45.

Bergson, Henri. *Time and Free Will: An Essay on the Immediate Data of Consciousness*. Trans. F. L. Pogson. 1910; rpt. New York, 1960.

———. *The Creative Mind: An Introduction to Metaphysics*. Trans. Mabelle L. Andison. New York, 1946.

Binkley, Timothy. "On the Truth and Probity of Metaphor." In *Philosophical Perspectives on Metaphor*, 136–53. *See* Mark Johnson.

Black, Max. *Models and Metaphors*. Ithaca, 1962.

———. "How Do Pictures Represent?" In *Art, Perception, and Reality*. E. H. Gombrich, Julian Hochberg, and Max Black, 95–129. Baltimore, 1972.

———. "How Metaphors Work: A Reply to Donald Davidson." In *On Metaphor*, 181–92. *See* Sacks.

———. "More About Metaphor." In *Metaphor and Thought*, 19–43. *See* Ortony.

Blanchot, Maurice. *The Sirens' Song: Selected Essays by Maurice Blanchot*. Ed. Gabriel Josipovici. Trans. Sacha Rabinovitch. Bloomington, 1982.

Blandshard, Brand. *The Nature of Thought*. 2 vols. London, 1939.

———. *Reason and Analysis*. La Salle, 1964.

Blumenberg, Hans. "The Life-World and the Concept of Reality." In *Life-World and Consciousness: Essays for Aron Gurwitsch*, 425–44. *See* Embree.

Booth, Wayne C. "Metaphor as Rhetoric: The Problem of Evaluation." In *On Metaphor*, 47–70. *See* Sacks.

———. "Pluralism in the Classroom." *Critical Inquiry* 12 (1986): 468–79.

Brown, Frank Burch. *Transfiguration: Poetic Metaphor and the Language of Religious Belief*. Chapel Hill, 1983.

Bruner, Jerome S. "Myth and Identity." In *Myth and Mythmaking*, 276–87. *See* Henry Murray.

Casey, Edward. S. *Imagining: A Phenomenological Study*. Bloomington, 1976.

Cassirer, Ernst. *The Philosophy of Symbolic Forms*. Trans. Ralph Manheim. 3 vols. New Haven, 1955–57.

———. *An Essay on Man*. 1944; rpt. New Haven, 1976.

———. *Language and Myth*. Trans. Susanne Langer. 1946; rpt. New York, 1953.

———. *The Logic of the Humanities*. Trans. Clarence Smith Howe. New Haven, 1961.

———. *Symbol, Myth, and Culture: Essays and Lectures of Ernst Cassirer 1935–1945*. Ed. Donald Phillip Verene. New Haven, 1979.

Chatman, Seymour, and Samuel R. Levin, eds. *Essays on the Language of Literature*. Boston, 1967.

Cohen, Morris R. *A Preface to Logic*. 1944; rpt. New York, 1977.

Cohen, Ted. "Metaphor and the Cultivation of Intimacy." In *On Metaphor*, 1–10. *See* Sacks.

Croce, Benedetto. *Aesthetic as Science of Expression and General Linguistic*. 2d ed. Trans. Douglas Ainslie. 1922; rpt. London, 1929.

cummings, e. e. *50 Poems*. New York, 1940.

Dallmayr, Fred. R. *Twilight of Subjectivity: Toward a Post-Individualist Theory of Politics*. Amherst, 1981.

Danto, Arthur, and Sidney Morgenbesser, eds. *Philosophy of Science*. Cleveland, 1960.

Davidson, Donald. "What Metaphors Mean." In *On Metaphor*, 29–45. *See* Sacks.

Davies, Stephen. "Truth-Value and Metaphor." *Journal of Aesthetics and Art Criticism* 42 (1984): 291–302.

Dempster, Douglas J. "Aesthetic Experience and Psychological Definitions of Art." *Journal of Aesthetics and Art Criticism* 44 (1985): 153–65.

Denham, Robert D. *Northrop Frye and Critical Method*. University Park, PA, 1978.

Derrida, Jacques. *Margins of Philosophy*. Trans. Alan Bass. Chicago, 1982.

Dewey, John. *Art as Experience*. 1934; rpt. New York, 1958.

Dickinson, Emily. *The Complete Poems of Emily Dickinson*. Ed. Thomas H. Johnson. Boston, 1960.

Dubois, J., et al. *A General Rhetoric*. Trans. Paul B. Burrell and Edgar M. Slotkin. Baltimore, 1981.

Eco, Umberto. "The Scandal of Metaphor: Metaphorology and Semiotics." *Poetics Today* 4 (1983): 217–57.

Edie, James. "Identity and Metaphor: A Phenomenological Theory of Polysemy." *Journal of the British Society for Phenomenology* 6 (1975): 32–41.

———. "Appearance and Reality: An Essay on the Philosophy of the Theatre." *Philosophy and Literature* 4 (1980): 3–17.

Elledge, Scott. *Milton's "Lycidas."* New York, 1966.

Embree, Lester, E., ed. *Life-World and Consciousness: Essays for Aron Gurwitsch.* Evanston, 1972.

Emerson, Ralph Waldo. "The Poet." In *The Collected Works of Ralph Waldo Emerson.* Ed. Joseph Slater et al. Cambridge, MA, 1971–. Vol. 3, 1–24.

Falk, Eugene H. *The Poetics of Roman Ingarden.* Chapel Hill, 1981.

Feagin, Susan L. "Some Pleasures of Imagination." *Journal of Aesthetics and Art Criticism* 43 (1985): 41–55.

Finke, Ronald A. "Mental Imagery and the Visual System." *Scientific American* 254.3 (1986): 88–95.

Foss, Martin. *Symbol and Metaphor in Human Experience.* Princeton, 1949.

Frisch, Max. *Homo Faber.* Trans. Michael Bullock. New York, 1959.

Frye, Northrop. *Anatomy of Criticism: Four Essays.* Princeton, 1957.

———. *Fables of Identity: Studies in Poetic Mythology.* New York, 1963.

———. *The Educated Imagination.* Bloomington, 1964.

Gadamer, Hans-Georg. *Philosophical Hermeneutics.* Ed. and trans. David E. Linge. Berkeley, 1976.

Garnett, A. Campbell. *Reality and Value: An Introduction to Metaphysics and an Essay on the Theory of Value.* New Haven, 1937.

Geertz, Clifford. *Local Knowledge: Further Essays in Interpretive Anthropology.* New York, 1983.

Gelvin, Michael. "Language as Saying and Showing." *Journal of Value Inquiry* 17 (1983): 151–63.

Goodheart, Eugene. *The Skeptic Disposition in Contemporary Criticism.* Princeton, 1984.

Goodman, Nelson. *Languages of Art: An Approach to a Theory of Symbols.* 2d ed. Indianapolis, 1976.

———. *Ways of Worldmaking.* Indianapolis, 1978.

———. "Metaphor as Moonlighting." In *On Metaphor,* 175–80. *See* Sacks.

Gumpel, Liselotte. *Metaphor Reexamined: A Non-Aristotelian Perspective.* Bloomington, 1984.

Gurwitsch, Aron. *The Field of Consciousness.* Pittsburgh, 1964.

———. "Philosophical Presuppositions of Logic." Trans. Abigail L. Rosenthal. In *Studies in Phenomenology and Psychology.* Evanston, 1966. 350–58.

Hagopin, John V. "Symbol and Metaphor in the Transformation of Reality into Art." *Comparative Literature* 20 (1968): 45–54.

Hamburger, Käte. *The Logic of Literature.* 2d ed. Trans. Marilynn J. Rose. Bloomington, 1973.

Harré, Rom. *The Philosophies of Science: An Introductory Survey.* New York, 1972.

Harries, Karsten. "Metaphor and Transcendence." In *On Metaphor,* 71–88. *See* Sacks.

Hartman, Charles O. "Cognitive Metaphor." *New Literary History* 13 (1982): 329–38.

Hartman, Geoffrey. *Easy Pieces*. New York, 1985.

Hawkes, Terence. *Metaphor*. 1972; rpt. London, 1977.

Herbert, George. *The English Poems of George Herbert*. Ed. C. A. Patrides. London, 1974.

Hesse, Mary. *Revolutions and Reconstructions in the Philosophy of Science*. Bloomington, 1980.

Hester, Marcus. B. *The Meaning of Poetic Metaphor: An Analysis in the Light of Wittgenstein's Claim That Meaning Is Use*. The Hague, 1967.

Hill, Knox C. *Interpreting Literature*. Chicago, 1966.

Hirsch, E. D. *Validity in Interpretation*. New Haven, 1967.

———. "On Theories and Metaphors: A Comment on Mary Hesse's Paper." *New Literary History* 18 (1985): 49–55.

Holdheim, W. Wolfgang. "Wilhelm Worringer and the Polarity of Understanding." In *The Question of Textuality: Strategies of Reading in Contemporary American Criticism*. Ed. William V. Spanos, Paul A. Bove, and Daniel O'Hara. Bloomington, 1982.

Hrushovski, Benjamin. "An Outline of Integrational Semantics." *Poetics Today* 3 (1982): 59–88.

———. "Poetic Metaphor and Frames of Reference." *Poetics Today* 5 (1984): 5–43.

Husserl, Edmund. *Ideas: General Introduction to Pure Phenomenology*. Trans. W. R. Boyce Gibson. 1931; rpt. New York, 1975.

Ihde, Don. *Consequences of Phenomenology*. Albany, 1986.

Iser, Wolfgang. *The Act of Reading: A Theory of Aesthetic Response*. Baltimore, 1978.

James, Henry. *The Golden Bowl*. Vols. 23 and 24 of *The Novels and Tales of Henry James*. New York edition. New York, 1909.

James, William. *Psychology: The Briefer Course*. Ed. Gordon Allport. New York, 1961.

———. *A Pluralistic Universe*. Ed. Frederick Burkhardt, Fredson Bowers, and Ignas Skrupskelis. Cambridge, MA, 1977.

Johnson, A. H. *Whitehead's Theory of Reality*. 1952; rpt. New York, 1962.

Johnson, Mark, ed. *Philosophical Perspectives on Metaphor*. Minneapolis, 1981.

Kaplan, Bernard. "Radical Metaphor, Aesthetics, and the Origin of Language." *Review of Existential Psychology and Psychiatry* 2 (1962): 75–84.

Kaufmann, Fritz. "Cassirer, Neo-Kantianism, and Phenomenology." In *The Philosophy of Ernst Cassirer*, 799–854. *See* Schilpp.

Kaufmann, Walter. *Nietzsche: Philosopher, Psychologist, Antichrist*. 3d ed. Princeton, 1968.

———. *Tragedy and Philosophy*. Garden City, 1968.

Kinney, Arthur F. *Faulkner's Narrative Poetics: Style as Vision*. Amherst, 1978.

Koestler, Arthur, and J. R. Smythies. *Beyond Reductionism: New Perspectives in the Life Sciences*. New York, 1969.

Lakoff, George, and Mark Johnson. "Conceptual Metaphor in Everyday Language." In *Philosophical Perspectives on Metaphor*, 286–325. *See* Mark Johnson.

———. *Metaphors We Live By*. Chicago, 1980.

Langer, Susanne. "On Cassirer's Theory of Language and Myth." In *The Philosophy of Ernst Cassirer*, 381–400. *See* Schilpp.

———. *Feeling and Form: A Theory of Art Developed From "Philosophy in a New Key."* New York, 1953.

————. *Philosophy in a New Key: A Study in the Symbolism of Reason, Rite, Art*. 3d ed. 1957; rpt. Cambridge, MA, 1980.

————. *Problems of Art*. New York, 1957.

————. *Mind: An Essay on Human Feeling*. 3 vols. Baltimore, 1967–82.

Lauer, Quentin. *Phenomenology: Its Genesis and Prospect*. 1958; rpt. New York, 1965.

Leclerc, Ivor. *Whitehead's Metaphysics*. Bloomington, 1975.

Lentricchia, Frank. *After the New Criticism*. Chicago, 1980.

Levin, Samuel R. *The Semantics of Metaphor*. Baltimore, 1977.

————. "Standard Approaches to Metaphor and a Proposal for Literary Metaphor." In *Metaphor and Thought*, 124–35. *See* Ortony.

Lewis, C. I. *An Analysis of Knowledge and Valuation*. La Salle, 1946.

————. *Collected Papers of Clarence Irving Lewis*. Ed. John D. Goheen and John L. Mothershead, Jr. Stanford, 1970.

Lonergan, Bernard J. F. *Insight: A Study of Human Understanding*. 1958; rpt. San Francisco, 1978.

MacCormac, Earl R. *A Cognitive Theory of Metaphor*. Cambridge, MA, 1985.

Martin, Robert Bernard. *Tennyson: The Unquiet Heart*. Oxford, 1980.

Melville, Herman. *Mardi, and a Voyage Thither*. Vol. 3 of *The Writings of Herman Melville*. Northwestern-Newberry Edition. Ed. Harrison Hayford, Hershel Parker, and G. Thomas Tanselle. Evanston, 1968–.

Merleau-Ponty, Maurice. "What is Phenomenology?" Trans. Colin Smith. In *The Essential Writings of Merleau-Ponty*. Ed. Alden L. Fisher. New York, 1969, 27–43.

————. "An Unpublished Text by Maurice Merleau-Ponty: A Prospectus of His Work." Trans. Arleen B. Dallery. In *The Essential Writings*, 367–76.

Miall, David S., ed. *Metaphor: Problems and Perspectives*. Atlantic Highlands, NJ, 1982.

Miller, Donald F. "Metaphor, Thinking, and Thought." *Et Cetera* 39 (1982): 134–50.

Miller, Jonathan. "The Mind's Eye and the Human Eye." *Daedalus* 114.4 (1985): 185–99.

Milton, John. *John Milton: Complete Poems and Major Prose*. Ed. Merrit Y. Hughes. Indianapolis, 1957.

Moneta, Giuseppina Chiara. "The Foundation of Predicative Experience and the Spontaneity of Consciousness." In *Life-World and Consciousness*, 171–90. *See* Embree.

Morris, Charles. *Signification and Significance: A Study of the Relations of Signs and Values*. Cambridge, MA, 1964.

Murray, Henry A., ed. *Myth and Mythmaking*. Boston, 1968.

Murray, John Middleton. "Metaphor." In *Essays on Metaphor*, 27–39. *See* Shibles.

Nagel, Ernest. "The Meaning of Reduction in the Natural Sciences." In *Philosophy of Science*, 288–312. *See* Danto and Morgenbesser.

Natanson, Maurice, ed. *Essays in Phenomenology*. The Hague, 1966.

Newman, Charles. *The Post-Modern Aura: The Act of Fiction in an Age of Inflation*. Evanston, 1985.

Norton, David. *Personal Destinies: A Philosophy of Ethical Individualism*. Princeton, 1976.

Novitz, David. "Metaphor, Derrida, and Davidson." *Journal of Aesthetics and Art Criticism* 44 (1985): 101–14.

Olsen, Stein Haugom. *The Structure of Literary Understanding*. Cambridge, 1978.

————. "Understanding Literary Metaphor." In *Metaphor: Problems and Perspectives*, 36–54. *See* Miall.

Ong, Walter J. *Rhetoric, Romance and Technology: Studies in the Interaction of Expression and Culture*. Ithaca, 1971.

————. *Interfaces of the Word: Studies in the Evolution of Consciousness and Culture*. Ithaca, 1977.

Ortony, Andrew, ed. *Metaphor and Thought*. Cambridge, 1979.

————. "The Role of Similarity in Similes and Metaphors." In *Metaphor and Thought*, 186–201. *See* Ortony.

Palmer, F. R. *Semantics: A New Outline*. London, 1976.

Palmer, Richard E. *Hermeneutics: Interpretation Theory in Schleiermacher, Dilthey, Heidegger, and Gadamer*. Evanston, 1969.

Parker, Patricia A. "The Metaphorical Plot." In *Metaphor: Problems and Perspectives*, 133–57. *See* Miall.

Percy, Walker. "Metaphor as Mistake." In *The Message in the Bottle: How Queer Man Is, How Queer Language Is, and What One Has To Do with the Other*. New York, 1975.

Pirsig, Robert M. *Zen and the Art of Motorcycle Maintenance*. New York, 1974.

Polanyi, Michael. *The Tacit Dimension*. New York, 1966.

————, and Harry Prosch. *Meaning*. Chicago, 1975.

Popper, Karl. *Unended Quest: An Intellectual Autobiography*. La Salle, 1976.

————. "Philosophical Comments on Tarski's Theory of Truth." In *Objective Knowledge: An Evolutionary Approach*. Rev. ed. Oxford, 1979, 319–40.

Putnam, Daniel A. "Music and the Metaphor of Touch." *Journal of Aesthetics and Art Criticism* 49 (1985): 59–66.

Quine, W. V. *From a Logical Point of View: 9 Logico-Philosophical Essays*. 2d. ed. New York, 1961.

————. *Ontological Relativity and Other Essays*. New York, 1969.

Read, Herbert. *The Forms of Things Unknown: Essays Towards an Aesthetic Philosophy*. New York, 1960.

Richards, I. A. *The Philosophy of Rhetoric*. Oxford, 1936.

Ricoeur, Paul. *The Rule of Metaphor: Multidisciplinary Studies of the Creation of Meaning in Language*. Trans. Robert Czerny with Kathleen McLaughlin and John Costello. Toronto, 1977.

————. "The Metaphorical Process as Cognition, Imagination, Feeling." In *On Metaphor*, 141–57. *See* Sacks.

————. *Time and Narrative*. 2 vols. to date. Trans. Kathleen McLaughlin and David Pellauer. Chicago, 1984–85.

Riffaterre, Michael. *Semiotics of Poetry*. Bloomington, 1978.

Rorty, Richard. *Philosophy and the Mirror of Nature*. Princeton, 1979.

Rosen, Stanley. *G. W. F. Hegel: An Introduction to the Science of Wisdom*. New Haven, 1974.

————. *The Limits of Analysis*. New York, 1980.

Rosmarin, Adena. "Theory and Practice: From Ideally Separated to Pragmatically Joined." *Journal of Aesthetics and Art Criticism* 43 (1984):31–40.

Sacks, Sheldon, ed. *On Metaphor*. Chicago, 1978.

Santayana, George. *Little Essays: Drawn from the Writings of George Santayana*. Ed. Logan Pearsall Smith and George Santayana. New York, 1920.

———. "Literal and Symbolic Knowledge." In *Obiter Scripta: Lectures, Essays, and Reviews*. Ed. Justus Buchler and Benjamin Schwartz. New York, 1936, 108–50.

Sartre, Jean-Paul. *Literature and Existentialism*. Trans. Bernard Frechtman. New York, 1964.

———. *Essays in Existentialism*. Ed. Wade Baskin. Secaucus, 1974.

———. *Psychology of Imagination*. Secaucus, n.d.

Scheffler, Israel. *Beyond the Letter: A Philosophical Inquiry into Ambiguity, Vagueness and Metaphor in Language*. London, 1979.

Schilpp, Paul Arthur, ed. *The Philosophy of Ernst Cassirer*. 1949; rpt. La Salle, 1973.

Scholes, Robert. *Textual Power: Literary Theory and the Teaching of English*. New Haven, 1985.

Schorer, Mark. "The Necessity of Myth." In *Myth and Mythmaking*, 354–58. See Henry Murray.

Searle, John R. "What is a Speech Act?" In *The Philosophy of Language*. Ed. J. R. Searle. London, 1971, 39–53.

———. *Expression and Meaning: Studies in the Theory of the Speech Acts*. Cambridge, 1979.

———. "Metaphor." In *Metaphor and Thought*, 92–123. See Ortony.

Searle, Roger. "Metaphors: Live, Dead, and Silly." In *The Play of Language*. Ed. Leonard F. Dean, Walker Gibson, and Kenneth G. Wilson. New York, 1971.

Sherburne, Donald W. *A Key to Whitehead's PROCESS AND REALITY*. 1966; rpt. Bloomington, 1975.

Shibles, Warren A. *An Analysis of Metaphor in the Light of W. M. Urban's Theories*. The Hague, 1971.

———, ed. *Metaphor: An Annotated Bibliography*. Whitewater, WI, 1971.

———, ed. *Essays On Metaphor*. Whitewater, WI, 1972.

Sidney, Philip. "The Defence of Poesie." In *The Complete Works of Sir Philip Sidney*. Ed. Albert Feuillerat. Cambridge, 1922–23. Vol. 3, 3–46.

Sinclair, Angus. *The Conditions of Knowing: An Essay Toward a Theory of Knowledge*. New York, 1951.

Sircello, Guy. "The Poetry of Theory: Reflections on *After the New Criticism*." *Journal of Aesthetics and Art Criticism* 4 (1984): 387–96.

Slochower, Harry. "Ernst Cassirer's Functional Approach to Art and Literature." In *The Philosophy of Ernst Cassirer*, 633–59. See Schilpp.

Spariosu, Mihai, ed. *Mimesis in Contemporary Theory: An Interdisciplinary Approach, Volume I: The Literary and Philosophical Debate*. Philadelphia, 1984.

Stambovsky, Phillip A. "Emily Dickinson's 'The Last Night That She Lived': Explorations of a Witnessing Spirit." *Concerning Poetry* 19 (1986): 87–93.

Stanford, W. B. *Greek Metaphor: Studies in Theory and Practice*. Oxford, 1936.

Stern, Laurent. "Hermeneutics and Intellectual History." *Journal of the History of Ideas* 46 (1985): 287–96.

Stevens, Wallace. "Effects of Analogy." In *The Necessary Angel: Essays on Reality and the Imagination*. New York, 1951, 105–30.

————. *The Collected Poems of Wallace Stevens*. New York, 1954.

Strasser, Stephan. *Understanding and Explanation: Basic Ideas Concerning the Humanities of the Human Sciences*. Pittsburgh, 1985.

Tarski, Alfred. "The Concept of Truth in Formalized Language." In *Logic, Semantics, Mathematics: Papers from 1923–1938*. Trans. J. H. Woodger. Oxford, 1956, 152–278.

Tatarkiewicz, W. "Mimesis." In *Dictionary of the History of Ideas*. Ed. Philip P. Weiner. New York, 1973. Vol. 3, 225–30.

Tate, Allen. *Collected Poems: 1919–1976*. New York, 1977.

Todorov, Tzvetan. *Theories of the Symbol*. Trans. Catherine Porter. Ithaca, 1982.

Tourangeau, Roger. "Metaphor and Cognitive Structure." In *Metaphor: Problems and Perspectives*. See Miall.

Ullman, Stephen. *Semantics: An Introduction to the Science of Meaning*. New York, 1979.

Urban, Wilbur Marshall. *Language and Reality: The Philosophy of Language and the Principles of Symbolism*. 1939; rpt. New York, 1971.

————. "Cassirer's Philosophy of Language." In *The Philosophy of Ernst Cassirer*, 403–41. See Schilpp.

Verene, Donald Phillip. *Vico's Science of Imagination*. Ithaca, 1981.

Wellek, Rene, and Austin Warren. *Theory of Literature*. 2d ed. New York, 1956.

Welsh, Paul. "Discourse and Presentational Symbols." *Mind* n.s. 64 (1955): 181–99.

Werkmeister, William H. "Cassirer's Advances Beyond Neo-Kantianism." In *The Philosophy of Ernst Cassirer*, 759–98. See Schilpp.

Wheelwright, Philip. *Metaphor and Reality*. Bloomington, 1962.

White, Hayden. *Tropics of Discourse: Essays in Cultural Criticism*. Baltimore, 1978.

Whitehead, Alfred North. *Symbolism: Its Meaning and Effect*. 1927; rpt. New York, 1959.

————. *Modes of Thought*. 1938; rpt. New York, 1968.

————. *Process and Reality; Corrected Edition*. Ed. David Ray Griffin and Donald W. Sherburne. New York, 1978.

Wittgenstein, Ludwig. *Tractatus Logico-Philosophicus*. Trans. D. F. Pears and B. F. McGuinness. 1961; rpt. London, 1974.

Yoos, George E. "A Phenomenological Look at Metaphor." *Philosophy and Phenomenological Research* 32 (1971): 78–88.

Young, Robert, ed. *Untying the Text: A Post-Structuralist Reader*. Boston, 1981.

Ziolkowski, Theodore. *Disenchanted Images: A Literary Iconology*. Princeton, 1977.

INDEX

Narrative development in *The Golden Bowl*, 78–84

Narrative imagery. *See* Literary image

Newman, Charles: criticism vs aesthetic consciousness, 137 n.32; *The Post-Modern Aura*, 133 n.52

Nietzsche, Friedrich, on literary decadence, 128 n.19

Northrop, F. S. C., *The Logic of the Sciences and the Humanities*, 121 n.40, 126 n.12

Norton, David, 57; *Personal Destinies*, 130 n.35

Novitz, David, "Metaphor, Derrida, and Davidson," 137 n.29

Obiter Scripta (Santayana), 85, 131 n.45

Objective Knowledge (Popper), 43–44, 123 n.62

Ogden, C. K., 94

Olsen, Stein Haugom, *The Structure of Literary Understanding*, 124 n.67

"On Theories and Metaphors" (Hirsch), 137 n.39

"On the Truth and Probity of Metaphor" (Binkley), 36

Ong, Walter J., 16, 42; *Interfaces of the Word*, 119 n.23; "Literate Orality and Popular Culture," 43

Ortony, Andrew, "The Role of Similarity in Simile and Metaphor," 118 n.14

"Outline of Integrational Semantics, An" (Hrushovski), 36, 105, 126 n.10

Palmer, Richard E., *Hermeneutics*, 126 n.9, 133 n.50

Participatory enactment, 58. *See also* Enactive envisagement

Peirce, C. S., 29

Pepper, Stephen C., *World Hypotheses*, 122 n.52

Percy, Walker, "Metaphors as Mistake," 14

Personal Destinies (Norton), 130 n.35

Perspective in Whitehead's Metaphysics (Ross), 129 n.28

Phenomenological analysis, 45–69, 95–100

"Phenomenological Look at Metaphor, A" (Yoos), 8, 20, 26, 95–99, 108, 119 n.29, 136 nn.27, 29, 137 n.30

Phenomenology (Lauer), 125 n.1

"Phenomenology, 'Metaphor-Metaphysics' and the Text" (Ihde), 137 n.34

Phenomenology of Knowledge (Cassirer), 77–78, 134 n.56, 135 n.6

Phenomenology of Perception, The (Merleau-Ponty), 125 n.1

Philosophical Hermeneutics (Gadamer), 42

Philosophical Perspectives on Metaphor (Mark Johnson), 5, 11, 17–20, 24, 27–30, 35–37, 116 nn.8, 3, 117 n.9, 120 n.32, 136 n.26

Philosophies of Science, The (Harré), 118 n.12

Philosophy and the Mirror of Nature (Rorty), 106, 136 n.28

Philosophy in a New Key (Langer), 129 n.27

Philosophy of Rhetoric, The (Richards), 17, 21–22, 34, 97

Philosophy of Symbolic Forms, The (Cassirer), 77–78, 105–6, 134 n.56, 135 nn.6, 11

Pirsig, Robert M., *Zen and the Art of Motorcycle Maintenance*, 60–61, 63–64, 86

"Pluralism in the Classroom" (Booth), 134 n.58

Pluralistic Universe, A (William James), 128 n.16

"Poet, The " (Emerson), 68, 134 n.57

"Poetic Metaphor and Frames of Reference" (Hrushovski), 14, 16, 115 n.2, 118 n.15, 119 nn.22, 24, 25, 122 nn.50, 56, 58

Poetics (Aristotle), 10–11

"Poetry and Grammaticalness" (Levin), 123 n.65

Polanyi, Michael, and Harry Prosch, *Meaning*, 26, 125 n.6

Acknowledgment is made to the following publishers for permission to reprint selections from copyrighted material:

From *Homo Faber* by Max Frisch, copyright © 1959 by Michael Bullock. Reprinted by permission of Harcourt Brace Jovanovich, Inc.

"A Bird came down the Walk" and lines from "The Last Night that She Lived" reprinted by permission of the publishers and the Trustees of Amherst College from *The Poems of Emily Dickinson*, edited by Thomas H. Johnson, Cambridge, Mass.: The Belknap Press of Harvard University Press, Copyright 1951, © 1955, 1979, 1983 by The President and Fellows of Harvard College.

"The Motive for Metaphor" from Wallace Stevens, *The Collected Poems of Wallace Stevens*, © 1954 by Wallace Stevens. Reprinted by permission of Alfred A. Knopf, Inc.

"Death of Little Boys" from *Collected Poems 1919–1976* by Allen Tate. Copyright © 1977 by Allen Tate. Reprinted by permission of Farrar, Straus and Giroux, Inc., and Faber and Faber Ltd.